CONQUER YOUR CHAOS

A Practical Guide to Boosting Productivity and Reducing Stress in the Digital Age

DEDICATION

This work is dedicated to:

- My mentors, for your invaluable guidance, wisdom, and for challenging me to reach my full potential. Your insights have shaped my journey in profound ways.
- My friends and family, for your constant support, encouragement, and understanding. Your presence in my life has made all the difference.
- The Almighty, for the blessings, strength, and opportunities that have guided my path. I am forever grateful for your grace.

Table of Content

Chapter	Title	Page No.
	Preface	1
	Introduction	3
1	Welcome to the Age of Overwhelm	5
2	Identifying Your Digital Distractions	18
3	From Productivity Drain to Mental Exhaustion	32
4	Defining Your Priorities	44
5	Mastering Your Time Management	55
6	Optimizing Your Digital Workspace	66
7	Cultivating a Growth Mindset	76
8	Implementing Healthy Habits	86
9	Maintaining Motivation and Avoiding Burnout	97
10	Crafting Your Action Plan	109
	Conclusion	121

Preface

The irony wasn't lost on me. Here I was, an author writing a book about conquering digital chaos, yet I myself constantly found myself battling the very monster I aimed to eliminate. Between overflowing inboxes, social media rabbit holes, and the constant buzz of notifications, my days often felt like a blur of fragmented attention and unfulfilled goals.

The frustration became a catalyst. I knew there had to be a better way. Driven by a desire for both personal transformation and a thirst to help others struggling with similar challenges, I embarked on a quest to reclaim control of my digital life.

This book is a culmination of that journey. It's a collection of the strategies and insights I gathered from research, experimentation, and conversations with countless individuals facing the same battle. It's not a theoretical treatise, but a practical guide, born from the trenches of digital overwhelm and strengthened with the hard-won lessons of experience.

This book is for you.
Whether you're drowning in emails, struggling to focus on work, or simply feeling overwhelmed by the constant demands of the digital age, this book offers a beacon of hope. Within these pages, you'll find the tools and strategies you need to conquer digital chaos and reclaim control of your time, attention, and well-being.

Consider this my confession and my calling. I confess to my own struggles with digital overwhelm, but I also extend a call to action: Let's conquer this together. Join me on this journey to a calmer, more productive, and fulfilling digital life.

Introduction

Drowning in Digital Overwhelm?
Take Control and Reclaim Your Time

Ever feel like you're constantly battling a never-ending inbox, a bottomless social media scroll, and a relentless stream of notifications? You're not alone. In today's hyper-connected world, digital overwhelm has become a common enemy, stealing our focus, draining our energy, and leaving us feeling overwhelmed and unproductive.

This book is your lifeline. We'll guide you on a journey to conquer digital chaos and reclaim control of your time. You'll discover powerful strategies to:

- **Tame the Inbox:** Learn to manage email overload and transform your inbox from a source of stress into a tool for efficiency.

- **Outsmart Distractions:** Identify and minimize digital distractions, allowing you to focus on deep work and achieve more in less time.

- **Master Prioritization:** Develop effective methods for prioritizing tasks, ensuring you're tackling the most important work first.

- **Embrace Self-Care:** Learn how to integrate healthy habits and mindfulness practices into your daily routine to combat stress and boost well-being.

- **Leverage Technology for Good:** Discover how to harness the power of technology to your advantage, utilizing productivity apps and tools to streamline your workflow and boost efficiency.

This book isn't just about getting things done; it's about living a more fulfilling life. By conquering digital chaos, you'll free up valuable time and mental space to focus on what truly matters – your passions, your relationships, and your overall well-being.

Ready to get rid of the overwhelm and embrace a calmer, more productive you? Let's dive in!

Chapter 1

Welcome to the Age of Overwhelm

This chapter dives deep into the ever-present challenge of digital overwhelm in our hyper-connected world. It explores the impact of the "always-on" culture and information overload, highlighting the negative consequences on our focus, well-being, and productivity.

The chapter opens with a relatable scenario of feeling overwhelmed by emails, notifications, and social media, emphasizing that this experience is common. It then introduces a quote by Cal Newport about the dangers of busywork without meaningful results.

Key elements covered:
- **The Always-On Culture:** This section describes the constant barrage of emails, messages, and social media updates that leave us feeling perpetually stressed and anxious.

- **Information Overload:** This section explores the issue of having access to more information than ever before, leading to decision fatigue and fragmented focus. Real-life examples illustrate the impact on professionals like Anu and David.

- **Taking Action:** A short quiz helps readers assess their level of digital overwhelm and directs them to relevant sections of the book based on their score.

- **The Productivity Paradox:** This section delves into the irony of having numerous productivity tools yet feeling less productive. It highlights the issues of feature creep and the distraction trap, using Jessica's example to showcase how complex tools can hinder progress.

- **The Cost of Chaos:** This section outlines the negative consequences of digital overwhelm on stress levels, well-being, and work performance. Mark's story demonstrates the impact on a sales director.

- **Actionable Tips:**
  - **Shine a Light on Your Digital Habits:** This section introduces a "Digital Detox Audit" as a way to track technology usage and identify areas for improvement.

  - **Unmask Your Digital Anxiety Triggers:** This section emphasizes the importance of recognizing personal triggers, like notification overload or FOMO, that contribute to stress. Sarah's story showcases the impact of constant email notifications on a lawyer.

The chapter concludes by encouraging readers to identify their digital anxieties and take the first step towards a calmer digital life through self-awareness.

Section:1

The Always-On Culture:
A Flood of Information, a Drowning Feeling

Remember that feeling on a Friday afternoon, when your inbox is overflowing, your phone keeps buzzing with notifications, and social media seems determined to suck you into an endless scroll?

You're not alone.
Welcome to the age of "*always-on*," where the digital world relentlessly demands our attention.

"The only thing worse than being busy is being busy doing nothing."
— Cal Newport

Think about it: emails pinging at all hours, work messages chasing us into the evening, and social media updates creating a constant pressure to stay connected. It's no wonder busy professionals like us often feel overwhelmed.

But here's the thing: This constant overflow is more than an unimportant irritation. It's a major contributor to the feeling of being perpetually overloaded. Studies show that the average office worker receives over 120 emails a day, and checks their phone upwards of 80 times! Imagine trying to focus on a complex report with that kind of digital white noise in the background. It's a recipe for stress, anxiety, and ultimately, decreased productivity.

Here's an example that might hit close to home:
Anu, a talented marketing professional, used to find herself constantly checking her email, even on weekends. The constant stream of messages left her feeling anxious and unsure if she was ever truly "off" work. This impacted her sleep, her ability to focus, and ultimately, the quality of her work. But by setting boundaries, like checking email only during specific times, and silencing notifications on her phone, Anu was able to reclaim control of her workday.

The point is, the "*always-on*" culture doesn't have to drown us. By recognizing its impact and taking steps to manage it, we can create a healthier, more productive work-life balance.

Section 2

Information Overload: Drowning in a Sea of Data

Remember that time you were researching a new client and ended up with dozens of open tabs, countless articles bookmarked, and still feeling unsure of the best approach? Information overload is a real problem in the digital age. We have access to more information than ever before, but that doesn't necessarily translate to better decision-making. In fact, the constant influx of data can have the opposite effect. Here's why:

- **Decision Fatigue:** Every decision, big or small, uses up our mental willpower. With the constant barrage of emails, news updates, and social media feeds, our decision-making muscles get tired. This can lead to a phenomenon called "decision fatigue," where we become less discerning and more likely to make poor choices or simply procrastinate altogether.

- **Focus Fragmentation:** Imagine trying to write a report while your phone keeps pinging with notifications and tempting headlines flash across your computer screen. That's the reality of information overload – it constantly disrupts our focus and makes it difficult to concentrate on any single task for a sustained period.

Here's a relatable example:
David, a software engineer, used to spend hours each morning sifting through endless news articles and industry blogs. While he felt like he was staying "informed," this constant information stream left him feeling overwhelmed and unable to focus on his actual work. By implementing a specific time for checking news and curating his information sources, David was able to regain control of his mornings and dedicate focused time to his coding projects.

The key takeaway? Information overload isn't just about the quantity of data – it's about the quality of our attention. By learning to manage information effectively, we can reclaim our focus and make better decisions in a world overflowing with data.

"The constant feeling of being overwhelmed or overloaded can contribute to a decline in mental and emotional well-being."
— Dr. Larry Rosen

Do you ever feel like you're drowning in emails, constantly bombarded by notifications, and struggling to keep up with the never-ending stream of information?

You're not alone!

Take this quick quiz to assess your current level of digital overwhelm and identify areas for improvement.

Instructions: Answer each question with "True" or "False."
1. I find it difficult to relax and disconnect from work in the evenings because I feel like I need to be available to check emails. (True/False)

2. I often lose track of time while scrolling through social media or browsing the internet. (True/False)

3. The constant buzz of notifications on my phone makes it hard for me to focus on tasks at work. (True/False)

4. I feel overwhelmed by the sheer number of unread articles and saved bookmarks I have accumulated online. (True/False)

5. I frequently experience anxiety or frustration when my internet connection is slow or unreliable. (True/False)

Scoring:
Give yourself 1 point for each question you answered "True."

- **0-1 points:** You might be experiencing mild digital overwhelm, but you're likely managing it fairly well.

- **2-3 points:** Digital distractions are impacting your focus and productivity to some extent. Consider implementing strategies to manage your technology use.

- **4-5 points:** You're likely experiencing significant digital overwhelm. This book can help you develop a plan to reclaim control and achieve a healthier digital balance.

Taking Action:
Based on your score, here are some sections of the book that might be particularly helpful for you:

- **Mild Overwhelm (0-1 points):**
    - Chapter 2: The Culprits of Chaos: Identifying Your Digital Distractions - Learn about common digital distractions and their impact on productivity.
    - Chapter 8: Implementing Healthy Habits for Peak Performance - Discover the importance of sleep, nutrition, and exercise for focus and well-being.

- **Moderate Overwhelm (2-3 points):**
    - Chapter 4: Defining Your Priorities: Setting Goals That Matter - Develop a clear understanding of your priorities and how to manage your time effectively.
    - Chapter 6: Optimizing Your Digital Workspace: Tools for Focus and Flow - Learn strategies for creating a distraction-free work environment and utilizing technology to your advantage.

- **Significant Overwhelm (4-5 points):**
    - Chapter 3: The Impact of Chaos: From Productivity Drain to Mental Exhaustion - Understand the negative consequences of digital overwhelm on your well-being and productivity.
    - Chapter 9: Maintaining Motivation and Avoiding Burnout - Discover techniques for managing stress, preventing burnout, and creating a sustainable work-life balance.

Remember, this is just a starting point. This book is designed to be a comprehensive guide to help you conquer your digital chaos and achieve a more focused and productive life!

Section: 3

The Productivity Paradox:
A Toolbox Overflowing, Yet Feeling Empty-Handed

Have you ever stared at a chaotic desk overflowing with fancy organizers, sticky notes, and color-coded pens, only to feel completely paralyzed about starting your next project? Welcome to the strange reality of the "Productivity Paradox." We're surrounded by more productivity tools and apps than ever before – to-do lists, time trackers, project management software – yet many of us feel less productive than ever.

Here's the irony:

- **Feature Creep:** Many productivity tools become bloated with features, creating a confusing learning curve and ultimately hindering efficiency. It's like having a toolbox overflowing with fancy gadgets, but not knowing how to use any of them!
- **The Distraction Trap:** Ironically, some productivity tools designed to help us focus can actually become distractions themselves. Just think about the endless notifications, pop-ups, and the siren call of social media lurking within those productivity apps.

Here's a relatable example:
Jessica, a project manager, used to spend hours meticulously planning her day in a complex project management software. However, the constant need to update tasks, categorize projects, and track progress became overwhelming. This time spent on "planning" actually

detracted from her ability to get actual work done. By simplifying her approach, using a basic to-do list app, and scheduling specific times for checking project management software, Jessica found she could focus on completing tasks, not just managing them.

The key takeaway? Don't get caught in the trap of believing more tools equal more productivity. Focus on finding the right tools that work for you, and use them strategically to streamline your workflow, not create additional clutter.

Section 4

The Cost of Chaos: From Overwhelm to Burnout

We've all been there – that feeling of drowning in emails, struggling to keep up with the constant stream of information, and feeling perpetually behind. But digital overwhelm isn't just a minor annoyance. It can have a significant impact on various aspects of our lives, including:

- **Stress Levels:** The constant pressure to be "on" can trigger the body's fight-or-flight response, leading to elevated cortisol (stress hormone) levels. This can manifest as feelings of anxiety, irritability, and difficulty sleeping.

- **Well-being:** Digital overload can take a toll on our mental and emotional well-being. Feeling overwhelmed can contribute to feelings of isolation, decreased motivation, and difficulty enjoying activities we once found pleasurable.

- **Work Performance:** Ironically, the very thing hindering our focus – digital clutter – can lead to decreased productivity at work. Constant distractions, information overload, and decision fatigue can make it difficult to concentrate on tasks and meet deadlines.

Here's a relatable example:
Mark, a sales director, used to check his work email constantly, even on evenings and weekends. This fear of missing out (FOMO) created a persistent feeling of anxiety and made it difficult for him to fully disconnect and recharge. This impacted his sleep, his ability to focus at work, and ultimately, his sales performance. By establishing clear boundaries between work and personal life, and scheduling specific times for checking email, Mark was able to reduce his stress levels and improve his overall performance.

The bottom line? Digital overwhelm isn't a badge of honour – it's a sign that something needs to change. By recognizing the negative impact, it can have on our well-being and productivity, we can take steps to reclaim control and create a healthier, more balanced digital life.

Actionable Tips: Shine a Light on Your Digital Habits
Ever feel like your phone is glued to your hand, or that your computer screen emits a tractor beam that pulls you in? The first step to reclaiming control from digital overwhelm is understanding your current habits. Here's a simple yet powerful technique: **Conduct a Digital Detox Audit!**

Think of it like a spring cleaning for your digital life.
For one entire day, track your technology usage. Here's how:

- **Download a Time Tracking App:** There are many free and paid apps available that can monitor your phone and computer usage. These will automatically track how much time you spend on different apps and websites.

- **The Pen and Paper Method:** For a low-tech approach, simply keep a notebook handy and jot down every time you pick up your phone or check your computer. Note the time, the app/website you accessed, and briefly describe what you were doing (e.g., "Checked work email," "Scrolled through social media").

Once you have a day's worth of data, analyse it! Look for patterns:
- **Time Sucks:** Which apps or websites are consuming the most time? Are there any social media rabbit holes you keep falling down?
- **Trigger Points:** Are there specific times of day when you find yourself mindlessly scrolling? Perhaps that first thing in the morning or during your lunch break?
- **The Interruption Monster:** How many times were you interrupted by notifications throughout the day? These constant dings and buzzes can be major productivity killers.

By understanding your digital habits, you can identify areas for improvement. **Think of it as a treasure map – a map that leads to a calmer, more focused you!**

This audit is just the first step. In the coming chapters, we'll explore powerful strategies to help you:

- **Set boundaries and reclaim control** of your digital life.
- **Harness the power of technology** to work for you, not against you.
- **Develop laser focus** and get things done without feeling overwhelmed.

So, grab your phone (ironically!), download that time tracking app, and let's get started on your digital detox journey!

Unmask Your Digital Anxiety Triggers
We've all been there – that sinking feeling in your stomach as your phone buzzes for the tenth time in an hour, or the rising tide of anxiety as your inbox overflows with unread messages. But what aspects of the digital world trigger these stress responses? Here's the key: **Recognize your stress triggers!**

Think about it like this: certain foods might trigger allergies in some people. Similarly, specific digital habits can trigger anxiety for busy professionals like you. Here's how to identify yours:

- **The Notification Nightmare:** Does the constant ping of notifications leave you feeling on edge and unable to focus? Perhaps it's the endless stream of work emails, or the barrage of social media updates.

- **The FOMO Frenzy:** Do you experience a fear of missing out (FOMO) when you're not constantly checking your social media feeds? The carefully curated online lives of others can fuel feelings of inadequacy and overwhelm.

- **The Information Avalanche:** Feeling constantly bombarded with news updates, industry blogs, and the pressure to stay "informed" can be a major stress trigger.

Here's a relatable example:
Mary, a lawyer, used to feel a surge of anxiety every time she saw the red notification bubble on her work email app. The constant pressure to be available and responsive was taking a toll on her well-being. By setting specific times for checking email and silencing notifications throughout the day, Mary was able to significantly reduce her stress levels and improve her focus.

Remember: Once you identify your digital anxiety triggers, you can start to develop strategies to manage them. In the coming chapters, we'll explore techniques like:
- **Setting boundaries** with your technology to create a calmer work environment.
- **Taming notifications** so they don't control your attention.
- **Developing healthy information consumption habits** to avoid information overload.

By understanding your stress triggers, you're taking the first step towards a more balanced and less anxiety-provoking digital life. So, grab a pen and paper, and start reflecting on what aspects of the digital world leave you feeling overwhelmed. The power to reclaim control starts with self-awareness!

Chapter 2

The Culprits of Chaos:
Identifying Your Digital Distractions

Welcome back to the journey of conquering digital overwhelms! In Chapter 1, we explored the ever-present struggle of information overload and the "always-on" culture. Now, it's time to delve deeper and identify the specific culprits behind your own digital distractions.

This chapter will act as a detective's guide, helping you uncover the hidden forces vying for your attention. We'll dissect the tactics employed by social media platforms to keep you hooked, expose the pitfalls of the "comparison trap," and shed light on the myth of multitasking.

But fret not, this won't be a mere diagnosis of the problem. We'll equip you with actionable tips to combat these distractions.

Here's a sneak peek of what awaits you in this chapter:

- **Understanding the Attention Economy:** Learn how social media platforms are designed to capture and hold your focus for as long as possible.

- **Breaking Free from the Comparison Trap:** Discover how social media's curated reality can negatively impact your self-esteem and explore strategies for building confidence.

- **Taming the Notification Frenzy:** Uncover the hidden costs of constant notifications and explore techniques to silence the digital chatter.

- **Debunking the Myth of Multitasking:** Learn why multitasking is a productivity killer and discover the power of focused work.

- **Taking Action:** We'll equip you with a toolbox of actionable tips, including:
    - A short quiz to identify your biggest digital distractors.
    - Strategies for scheduling focused work sessions and minimizing distractions.
    - Techniques to practice mindfulness and improve your ability to stay focused.
    - Examples of successful strategies implemented by others to overcome digital distractions.

By the end of this chapter, you'll be armed with the knowledge and tools to identify and conquer the digital distractions that are hindering your focus and productivity. Let's get started on reclaiming control of your time and attention!

Section 1

The Attention Economy: Captive Audience in the Digital Age

Welcome to the Attention Economy, a digital marketplace where our focus is the most valuable currency. Social media platforms and apps aren't just communication tools; they're sophisticated businesses designed to capture and hold our attention for as long as possible. Here's how they achieve this.

1. The Infinite Scroll: Gone are the days of paginated websites. Endless scrolling feeds on platforms like

Facebook, Instagram, and Twitter create the illusion of infinite content, encouraging us to keep swiping for that next dopamine hit.

2. The Notification Nation: The constant barrage of notifications – likes, comments, mentions – triggers a primal need to check and respond. These notifications act like tiny sirens, pulling us back into the app, even when we're trying to focus on other tasks.

3. The Algorithmic Magnetism: Social media platforms use complex algorithms to personalize our feeds, showing us content, they predict will keep us engaged. This "filter bubble" creates a sense of endless novelty, encouraging us to spend more time-consuming content that reinforces our existing beliefs and preferences.

4. The Gamification of Engagement: Features like badges, points, and streaks gamify the social media experience. These rewards trick our brains into associating the platform with positive reinforcement, making us crave the next virtual "win."

5. The Social Comparison Trap: Social media platforms are filled with carefully curated highlight reels of other people's lives. This constant comparison can fuel feelings of inadequacy and a desire to stay connected, keeping us glued to the screen.

The Impact on You:
These tactics are incredibly effective, and the consequences can be real. By constantly vying for our attention, social media platforms can:
- **Decrease Productivity:** The constant notifications and urge to check our feeds disrupt our

focus and makes it difficult to concentrate on deep work.

- **Increase Anxiety and FOMO:** The fear of missing out (FOMO) and the pressure to maintain a perfect online persona can contribute to anxiety and feelings of inadequacy.

- **Hamper Creativity:** The relentless stream of curated content can stifle our own creativity and independent thinking.

- **Damage Relationships:** Excessive social media use can take away from real-life interactions and damage our relationships with friends and family.

Remember: You're not alone. Social media platforms are designed to be addictive. However, by understanding their tactics, you can reclaim control and use them mindfully. The next chapter will explore strategies for managing social media distractions and establishing a healthier digital balance.

Section 2

The Comparison Trap:
Social Media's Curated Reality and Its Toll on Self-Esteem

Social media platforms are a highlight reel, showcasing the best vacations, the most delicious meals, and the happiest moments of other people's lives. But what we often forget is that these are carefully curated snapshots, not a reflection of everyday reality. Constantly comparing ourselves to these unrealistic portrayals can have a significant negative impact on our self-esteem and fuel feelings of inadequacy.

Here's how social media comparison can hurt:

- **The Distortion of Reality:** Social media feeds are filled with carefully edited photos and positive experiences. This creates an illusion of perfection that most people don't achieve in their daily lives. Believing this portrayal is the norm can make our own lives seem ordinary or lacking.

- **The Envy Equation:** Seeing others' successes and achievements can trigger feelings of envy and make it difficult to celebrate our own accomplishments. We may start focusing on what we lack instead of appreciating what we have.

- **The Insecurity Spiral:** Constant comparison can lead to social anxiety and insecurity. We may become overly concerned with how others perceive us online, leading to a cycle of self-doubt and negativity.

The Story of Shreya: From Comparison to Confidence

Shreya, a talented graphic designer, found herself constantly scrolling through social media, comparing her work to the seemingly flawless portfolios of other designers. This constant comparison left her feeling discouraged and unsure of her own abilities. However, by taking a break from social media and focusing on her own creative process, Shreya rediscovered her passion and developed a unique design style. She learned to celebrate her own creative journey, independent of online validation.

Remember: Social media is a highlight reel, not a documentary. Focus on your own life goals and celebrate your unique strengths and accomplishments. There's always someone who seems to have it "better," but true happiness comes from self-acceptance and appreciating your own journey.

Strategies Tips:
- **Schedule Focused Work Sessions:** Block out specific times in your calendar for focused work on a single task. Turn off notifications and silence your phone during these sessions. **Success Story:** Lisa, a busy marketing manager, implemented focused work sessions of 90 minutes each morning. During this time, she silenced all notifications and closed unnecessary browser tabs. This allowed her to concentrate on her most important marketing projects, significantly increasing her productivity.

- **Practice Mindfulness:** Mindfulness techniques can help you improve your ability to focus and resist distractions. Take a few minutes each day to practice mindful breathing or meditation. **Expert Tip:** According to mindfulness expert Jenny say, "Mindfulness helps us become aware of the present moment without judgment. This allows us to disengage from distracting thoughts and focus on the task at hand."

- **Utilize the Pomodoro Technique:** The Pomodoro Technique involves working in focused 25-minute intervals with short breaks in between. This method can help you maintain concentration and avoid burnout.

Taking Action:
- **Limit Social Media Consumption:** Set specific times for checking social media and stick to them. Consider taking breaks or even deleting social media apps from your phone for a period of time.

- **Practice Gratitude:** Focus on the positive aspects of your life. Start a gratitude journal and write down three things you're grateful for each day.

- **Celebrate Your Wins:** Take time to acknowledge your own accomplishments, big or small. Celebrate your progress and be proud of your unique journey.

- **Focus on Real Connections:** Nurture your relationships with friends and family who support and inspire you. Invest in real-life interactions that build you up, rather than online comparisons that bring you down.

Section 3

The Notification Frenzy: The Constant Buzz and its Productivity Drain

We've all been there: the never-ending ping of a new email, the flashing notification badge on our phone, the constant digital chatter contesting for our attention. While notifications may seem like harmless updates, the constant barrage can have a significant negative impact on our focus and productivity. Here's how:

- **The Interruption Monster:** Each notification, no matter how small, acts as an interruption. It pulls our attention away from the task at hand, forcing us to mentally shift gears. This constant context switching makes it difficult to concentrate on deep work and complete tasks efficiently.

- **The FOMO Frenzy:** The fear of missing out (FOMO) triggered by notifications can be a major productivity killer. We feel compelled to check every notification immediately, even if it's not urgent. This constant checking disrupts our workflow and prevents us from getting into a focused state.

- **The Multitasking Myth:** Our brains are not wired for true multitasking. When we switch our attention between tasks due to notifications, it actually decreases our overall productivity and increases the likelihood of errors.

The Case of John: Mastering Focus by Taming Notifications

John, a software engineer, used to keep his phone notifications turned on for all his apps. This constant stream of updates left him feeling overwhelmed and unable to focus on his coding projects. However, by implementing a system where he silenced all notifications except for urgent calls and texts, and scheduled specific times to check email and social media, John found he could concentrate on his work for longer stretches. This increase in focus led to a significant boost in his productivity.

Remember: Don't let notifications control your attention. By taking control of your notification settings, you can create a calmer and more focused work environment.

Actionable Tips:
- **Silence Notifications for Non-Essential Apps:** Turn off notifications for apps that are not critical for your work, such as social media or news apps.

- **Schedule Specific Check-In Times:** Set specific times throughout the day to check email and social media. This will help you avoid the constant urge to check for updates.

- **Utilize Focus Tools:** Several apps and browser extensions can help block distracting websites and apps during work hours.

- **Train Your Brain:** Practice mindfulness techniques to improve your ability to focus and resist distractions.

By following these tips, you can tame the notification frenzy and reclaim control of your workday.

Section 4

The Myth of Multitasking: Juggling or Dropping the Balls?

"Don't be afraid to give up the good to go for the great."
- John D. Rockefeller

We've all been there – trying to answer emails while on a call, writing a report while checking social media, or cooking dinner while catching up on the news. Multitasking feels like a badge of honour in our fast-paced world, a way to get more done in less time. However, the truth is that multitasking is a myth, and it can actually have a significant negative impact on your productivity. Here's why:

- **The Cost of Switching Gears:** Our brains are not designed to truly multitask. When we switch our attention between tasks, it takes time and mental energy to refocus. This "context switching" can slow us down significantly and lead to more errors. Imagine juggling multiple balls – you can keep a few in the air at once, but eventually, you'll drop one (or all of them!).

- **The Illusion of Efficiency:** While it may feel like you're accomplishing more by multitasking, you're actually spreading yourself thin. The quality of your work suffers when your attention is divided between multiple tasks. You may end up taking longer to complete each task and producing work with more mistakes.

- **The Productivity Paradox:** Studies show that multitasking can actually decrease your overall productivity by as much as 40%. The constant mental strain of switching between tasks leads to fatigue and decreased cognitive function.

Jessica's Multitasking Chaos:
Jessica, a marketing manager, believed she was a master multitasker. She would juggle answering emails, brainstorming campaign ideas, and attending conference calls all at once. However, she found herself feeling stressed, overwhelmed, and making more mistakes. When she finally implemented a system of focused work sessions, where she tackled one task at a time with minimal distractions, Jessica

discovered a significant boost in her productivity and creativity.

Remember: Focus is the key to true productivity. By prioritizing single-tasking and minimizing distractions, you can achieve more in less time and with better results.

Section 5

A Slice of Our Time:
Where Do Our Digital Minutes Go?

We all know we spend a significant amount of time online, but how much time are we dedicating to various digital activities? This pie chart titled "Breakdown of Time Spent on Digital Activities" offers a visual representation of where our digital minutes might be going. As you can see, the slices of the pie represent different categories of digital activities, with the largest slice indicating the most significant time commitment.

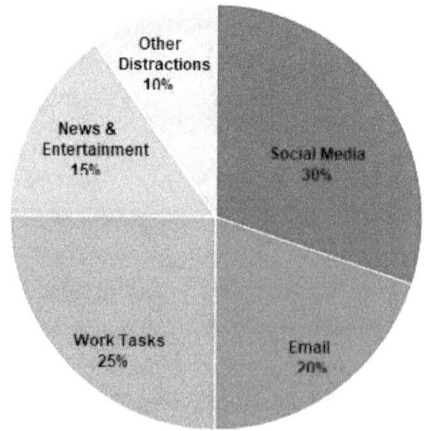

Breakdown of Time Spent on Digital Activities

Taking Control of the Pie: Insights from Our Digital Breakdown

The pie chart provides a snapshot of how our time might be distributed across various digital activities. While this is a general representation, it serves as a valuable starting point for self-reflection.

- **Social Media:** If the social media slice dominates the pie, it might be a good opportunity to consider strategies for managing social media use and setting boundaries.

- **Email:** A sizable email slice suggests the need for potential email management techniques to optimize workflow.

- **Other Distractions:** A smaller "other distractions" slice might still warrant exploration. Identifying what these distractions are can help you develop targeted strategies for minimizing their impact.

Remember, the goal is not to eliminate all digital activities, but to achieve a balance that supports your focus and productivity. By understanding how your time is currently spent, you can make informed choices about how to manage your digital world and reclaim control of your precious time.

"Time is more valuable than money. You can get more money, but you cannot get more time."
- Jim Rohn

Short Quiz: How Susceptible Are You to Digital Distractions?

Take this short quiz to identify your biggest digital distractors and gain insights into how technology might be impacting your focus and productivity.

Instructions: Answer each question with "Yes" or "No."
1. Do you find yourself checking your phone for notifications even when you're not expecting anything important?
2. Do you struggle to resist the urge to browse social media during work hours?
3. Do you ever feel overwhelmed by the constant stream of emails and messages?
4. Do you find it difficult to concentrate on a single task for extended periods due to digital interruptions?
5. Do you ever lose track of time while scrolling through news feeds or online content?

Scoring:
- **3 or more "Yes" answers:** Digital distractions are likely having a significant impact on your focus and productivity. The following sections in this chapter will provide you with actionable tips and strategies to manage your digital distractions and reclaim control of your time.
- **1-2 "Yes" answers:** Digital distractions may be impacting your focus to some extent. Consider implementing the tips in this chapter to minimize distractions and improve your ability to concentrate.
- **0 "Yes" answers:** Congratulations! You seem to have a good handle on digital distractions. However, it's always a good practice to be mindful of your technology use.

Actionable Tips:
- **Schedule Focused Work Sessions:** Block out specific times in your calendar for focused work on a single task. Turn off notifications and silence your phone during these sessions.

- **Practice Mindfulness:** Mindfulness techniques can help you improve your ability to focus and resist distractions. Take a few minutes each day to practice mindful breathing or meditation.

- **Utilize the Pomodoro Technique:** The Pomodoro Technique involves working in focused 25-minute intervals with short breaks in between. This method can help you maintain concentration and avoid burnout.

By breaking free from the myth of multitasking, you can unlock your true potential for focused, productive work.

Remember: You are not alone in the fight against digital distractions. By understanding the challenges and implementing the strategies outlined in this chapter, you can take back control of your time and focus on what truly matters.

Chapter 3

The Impact of Chaos:
From Productivity Drain to Mental Exhaustion

Welcome back to our journey of conquering digital overwhelms! In Chapter 2, we identified the culprits behind your digital distractions. Now, let's delve deeper and explore the significant consequences of this constant digital bombardment.

This chapter will showcase how digital chaos can wreak havoc on your well-being, impacting everything from your productivity to your sleep quality. But fear not, we'll also equip you with actionable tips and strategies to combat these negative effects and reclaim control.

Here's a sneak peek of what awaits you in this chapter:

- **The Stress Response:** We'll explore the physiological effects of chronic stress caused by digital overload, including cortisol release and decreased cognitive function.

- **Procrastination Paralysis:** We'll discuss how feeling overwhelmed can lead to procrastination and missed deadlines, featuring real-life examples of overcoming this challenge.

- **Anxiety Overload:** We'll explore the link between digital chaos and heightened anxiety levels, and how it can further impact your productivity and well-being.

- **The Importance of Sleep:** We'll explain how poor sleep quality, often disrupted by technology use, impacts focus and overall well-being.

- **Actionable Tips:**
    - A bar chart showcasing the "Impact of Digital Chaos on Productivity" (illustrating the decline in productivity due to stress, procrastination, and sleep deprivation).
    - Techniques to manage stress, such as deep breathing or meditation.
    - Strategies for creating a sleep schedule and avoiding screen time before bed.
    - Utilizing to-do list apps to break down large tasks into manageable steps to avoid feeling overwhelmed.

By the end of this chapter, you'll understand the detrimental effects of digital chaos and be armed with practical strategies to combat them. Let's dive in and take control of your digital world!

Section 1

The Stress Response:
When Chaos Makes Your Brain Go Haywire

Have you ever felt like you have a million tabs open in your mind – emails to answer, deadlines looming, social media notifications buzzing? This constant digital bombardment can trigger a real physiological response in your body called the stress response.

Fight or Flight... Freeze?

When faced with perceived threats (like an overflowing inbox or a never-ending to-do list), your body releases a surge of stress hormones, primarily cortisol. This hormone is designed to give you a burst of energy to deal with the immediate threat. Think of it as your body's built-in "fight or flight" response, preparing you for action.

The Problem with Chronic Chaos:

The problem with digital overwhelm is that it creates a state of chronic low-level stress. Your body is constantly releasing cortisol, even though there's no real physical danger. This chronic stress can have a significant impact on your brain and overall well-being.

Cortisol: The Productivity Zapper

Cortisol is a double-edged sword. While it can provide a short-term energy boost, chronically elevated levels can actually impair your cognitive function. Cortisol disrupts the production of new brain cells and weakens the hippocampus, the area of the brain responsible for memory and learning. This can lead to:

- **Difficulty concentrating:** Ever feel like you can't focus on a single task for more than a few minutes? Cortisol overload can make it hard to maintain focus and complete tasks efficiently.

- **Decision fatigue:** The constant barrage of choices and information overload can deplete your decision-making resources. Cortisol can make it even harder to make clear and sound decisions.

- **Reduced creativity:** Feeling stressed and overwhelmed isn't exactly a recipe for creative thinking. Cortisol can hinder your ability to generate new ideas and think outside the box.

Remember: Chronic stress isn't just bad for your productivity; it can also have a negative impact on your physical health. By managing digital distractions and reducing chronic stress, you're not just boosting your productivity, you're also taking care of your overall well-being.

Actionable Tip: Practice relaxation techniques like deep breathing or meditation for just a few minutes each day. These techniques can help to lower your stress response and improve your focus.

Manage Your Stress Response:
- **Practice Relaxation Techniques:** Deep breathing and meditation are powerful tools for managing stress. Deep breathing exercises like the 4-7-8 technique (inhale for 4 seconds, hold for 7 seconds, exhale for 8 seconds) can help to calm your nervous system and reduce anxiety. Meditation apps like Headspace or Calm can provide guided meditations for beginners.

Coming Up Next: We'll explore how feeling overwhelmed by digital chaos can lead to procrastination paralysis and missed deadlines.

Section 2

Procrastination Paralysis:
When Overwhelm Becomes Your Worst Enemy

Have you ever stared at a to-do list that seems to stretch as far as the eye can see, feeling paralyzed and unsure where to even begin? This is a classic symptom of "procrastination paralysis," a state triggered by the overwhelming feeling of digital chaos. Here's why:

The Burden of Choice: Imagine your inbox overflowing with emails, your project management tool bursting with tasks, and social media notifications constantly vying for your attention. This information overload creates a situation where simply deciding what to tackle first feels like an insurmountable hurdle.

Decision Fatigue: Our brains have a limited capacity for making decisions. The constant barrage of choices in the digital world depletes this decision-making resource. When faced with a seemingly endless to-do list, we might choose to avoid making any decisions at all, leading to procrastination.

The Fear of Failure: Feeling overwhelmed can fuel a fear of failure. When a project seems daunting or you're unsure where to start, the fear of not doing it well can lead to procrastination. We might tell ourselves, "I'll just do it later when I have more time" (which we probably won't!), putting the task off indefinitely.

The Case of Sarah: From Missed Deadlines to Masterful Management

Madhu, a marketing manager, constantly struggled with meeting deadlines. Her to-do list felt like a never-ending monster, and she found herself constantly bombarded by emails, notifications, and social media updates. This digital overwhelm led to procrastination and a cycle of missed deadlines and increased stress. However, by implementing strategies like breaking down large projects into smaller, more manageable tasks and scheduling focused work sessions with minimal distractions, Madhu transformed her workflow. She learned to prioritize tasks, tackle them one at a time, and finally conquered her procrastination paralysis.

Remember: Procrastination doesn't have to be your reality. By managing digital distractions and implementing effective time management techniques, you can break free from the cycle of overwhelm and become a master of getting things done.

Actionable Tip: Utilize to-do list apps that allow you to break down large projects into smaller, more manageable steps. This can help you feel less overwhelmed and make starting a task seem less daunting.

Conquer Your To-Do List:
- **Utilize To-Do List Apps:** Feeling overwhelmed by a never-ending to-do list can be paralyzing. To-do list apps like Todoist or Asana allow you to break down large projects into smaller, more manageable steps. This can help you feel less overwhelmed and make starting a task seem less daunting.

The Case of Michael: From Scattered to Strategic
Michael, a talented graphic designer, was drowning in a sea of digital chaos. His inbox overflowed with emails, his social media feeds buzzed with constant updates, and the allure of online games loomed large. This digital distraction made it nearly impossible for him to focus on his work. Deadlines loomed ever closer, his stress levels soared, and a good night's sleep felt like a distant dream.

The Cycle of Overwhelm:
Michael's workday was a constant battle against distractions. Every notification ping, every social media update, pulled him away from the task at hand. He'd start

working on a design project, only to get sidetracked by an urgent email (or not-so-urgent social media post). By the time he refocused on his work, precious time had been lost. The feeling of being overwhelmed made it difficult to prioritize tasks, leading to missed deadlines and a growing sense of frustration.

Taking Back Control:
Michael realized he needed to make a change. He started by implementing a few key strategies:

- **Taming the Inbox:** He set specific times for checking email, silencing notifications in between, and unsubscribing from unnecessary mailing lists.

- **Scheduling Social Media Breaks:** He allowed himself short, designated social media breaks throughout the day, but kept his phone on silent mode otherwise.

-
  Time Blocking for Focused Work: He blocked out specific time slots in his calendar for focused work on design projects, eliminating distractions during these critical periods.

- **Creating a Relaxing Sleep Routine:** Michael established a relaxing bedtime routine that included avoiding screens for at least an hour before bed and creating a sleep-conducive environment in his bedroom.

Reaping the Rewards:
By taking control of his digital world and setting boundaries, Michael's life transformed. He was able to focus on his work without constant distractions, completing projects on time and exceeding client expectations. Reduced stress levels led

to better sleep, further improving his focus and energy levels. Michael finally felt like he was in control of his workday, and his success as a designer soared.

This story illustrates the power of taking charge of your digital habits. By implementing effective time management techniques and setting boundaries, you can overcome procrastination paralysis, achieve a better work-life balance, and reach your full potential.

Coming Up Next: Let's explore the link between digital chaos and heightened anxiety levels, and how it can further impact your productivity and well-being.

Section 3

Anxiety Overload:
When Your Digital World Fuels Your Worries

Ever feel a sense of unease creeping in as you scroll through your social media feed or your inbox explodes with unread messages? It's not your imagination. Digital chaos can be a major contributor to heightened anxiety levels for busy professionals. Here's why:

The Constant Comparison Trap:
Social media platforms are filled with curated snapshots of other people's lives – the perfect vacations, the impressive promotions, the seemingly effortless achievements. Being bombarded with these unrealistic portrayals can trigger feelings of inadequacy and social comparison anxiety. We may start to worry that we're not measuring up, fueling a cycle of self-doubt and negativity.

The Fear of Missing Out (FOMO) Frenzy:
The constant stream of updates and notifications can create a pervasive fear of missing out (FOMO). We worry that if we disconnect for even a moment, we might miss something important – a crucial email, a game-changing industry update, or a hilarious meme (okay, maybe not that last one, but you get the idea!). This FOMO can lead to a constant state of low-level anxiety, making it difficult to relax and focus on the task at hand.

The Information Overload:
In today's digital age, we're bombarded with information from all sides. News alerts, breaking headlines, and a never-ending stream of emails can create a sense of information overload. This constant barrage can be overwhelming and contribute to feelings of anxiety, as we struggle to keep up and process everything.

The Case of Arun: From Anxious to Authentic
Arun, a software developer, used to constantly check his work email and social media feeds, even outside of work hours. This constant information stream fuelled his anxiety and made it difficult for him to truly disconnect and relax. However, by implementing strategies like setting specific times for checking email and social media, and scheduling digital detox breaks throughout the day, Arun significantly reduced his anxiety levels. He discovered the power of disconnecting and allowing himself time to recharge.

Remember: You don't have to be a slave to your digital devices. By managing your digital consumption and setting boundaries, you can break free from the anxiety trap and create a calmer, more focused work environment.

Actionable Tip: Schedule specific times for checking email and social media. Avoid checking these platforms first thing in the morning or right before bed, as this can contribute to anxiety.

Coming Up Next: We'll explore how poor sleep quality, often disrupted by technology use, can further impact your focus and overall well-being.

Section 4

The Importance of Sleep: When Your Phone Becomes Your Worst Bedfellow

We've all been there – tossing and turning at night, reaching for our phones "just for a quick check," only to find ourselves sucked into a social media vortex or lost in the abyss of work emails. This late-night digital indulgence can have a significant negative impact on your sleep quality, and as a consequence, your overall well-being and productivity. Here's why:

The Blue Light Blues: Most digital devices emit blue light, which can disrupt the production of melatonin, a hormone that regulates your sleep-wake cycle. Essentially, the blue light tricks your brain into thinking it's daytime, making it harder to fall asleep and stay asleep.

The Notification Nightmare: Let's be honest, the constant ping of notifications – emails, texts, social media updates – can be incredibly disruptive to a good night's sleep. Even if you're not actively checking your phone, the mere presence of those notifications can trigger anxiety and make it difficult to relax and drift off.

The Pre-Sleep Scroll: Scrolling through social media or checking work emails right before bed can stimulate your brain and make it hard to unwind. This pre-sleep screen time can leave you feeling wired and restless, further impacting your sleep quality.

The Power of a Power Nap: While aiming for 7-8 hours of sleep each night is ideal, busy professionals often find themselves short on time. Don't underestimate the power of a well-timed power nap! A 20-30 minute nap in the early afternoon can significantly improve your alertness, focus, and cognitive function, making you more productive throughout the day.

The Case of Jessica: From Sleepless to Successful
Jessica, a high-powered lawyer, constantly struggled with fatigue and difficulty focusing. She often worked late into the night, checking emails and responding to client calls, only to find herself exhausted and unproductive the next day. However, by implementing a sleep hygiene routine that included creating a relaxing bedtime ritual, avoiding screens for at least an hour before bed, and sticking to a consistent sleep schedule, Jessica significantly improved her sleep quality. This led to increased energy levels, sharper focus, and a boost in her overall productivity.

Remember: Prioritizing sleep isn't a luxury; it's a necessity for peak performance. By establishing healthy sleep habits and creating a screen-free sleep sanctuary, you can recharge your mind and body, and wake up feeling ready to conquer your workday.

Actionable Tip: Create a sleep schedule and stick to it as much as possible, even on weekends. This will help regulate your body's natural sleep-wake cycle.

Optimize Your Sleep for Peak Performance:
- **Create a Sleep Schedule:** Aim for 7-8 hours of sleep each night and try to go to bed and wake up at the same time each day, even on weekends. This consistency helps regulate your body's natural sleep-wake cycle.
- **Avoid Screen Time Before Bed:** The blue light emitted by electronic devices can disrupt your sleep cycle. Avoid using screens (phones, laptops, tablets) for at least an hour before bed. Instead, opt for relaxing activities like reading a book, taking a warm bath, or listening to calming music.

Bonus Tip: Schedule digital detox breaks throughout your day. Step away from your devices for short periods to disconnect and recharge. Take a walk in nature, stretch, or chat with a colleague – anything to give your mind a break from the constant digital stimulation.

Remember, these are just a few starting points. Experiment and find what works best for you. By implementing these actionable tips and taking control of your digital world, you can create a calmer, more focused, and ultimately, more productive work environment.

Chapter 4

Defining Your Priorities:
Setting Goals That Matter

Ever feel busy but unfulfilled? You're not alone! This chapter will help you set goals that truly matter to you. Think of your goals as a compass guiding you through life. We'll learn how to identify your core values, which are your guiding principles. Then, we'll explore a method called SMART goals to turn your dreams into action plans. Feeling overwhelmed by your to-do list? No worries! We'll cover prioritization techniques to help you focus on what's important. This chapter is packed with practical tips, exercises, and even templates to get you started. By the end, you'll have a roadmap to set meaningful goals, prioritize effectively, and live a life filled with purpose!

Section 1

The Power of Values:
Your Compass in the Chaos

Imagine you're lost in a dense forest, with a million paths branching out before you. Sure, you could wander aimlessly, hoping to stumble upon your destination. But wouldn't it be easier to have a compass – a guiding tool that helps you navigate towards a specific goal? Your core values act as that compass in the often-chaotic world of goal setting and decision-making.

What Are Core Values?

Your core values are the fundamental principles that guide your life – the things that are most important to you. They represent what you believe in and what you strive for. For example, some core values might be integrity, creativity, work-life balance, or continuous learning.

Why Are Core Values Important for Goal Setting?
When your goals are aligned with your core values, they become more meaningful and motivating. They give you a sense of purpose and direction, and they help you stay focused on what truly matters, even amidst the digital distractions of the modern world.

How to Identify Your Core Values:
- **Self-Reflection:** Take some quiet time to reflect on what truly matters to you in life. What are your non-negotiables? What qualities do you admire most in others? Journaling or mind-mapping exercises can be helpful for this process.

- **Life Experiences:** Consider the times in your life when you felt most fulfilled. What values were present in those situations? Conversely, think about times when you felt unfulfilled. What values were missing?

- **Role Models:** Who do you admire? What are their core values? Can you identify any values they embody that resonate with you?

The Value-Driven Decision Matrix:
Feeling overwhelmed by a sea of options? Create a simple decision matrix to help you make choices that align with your core values. List your core values on one axis and your potential options on the other. Rate each option based on how well it aligns with each value. This will help you identify

the choices that are most congruent with your overall direction.

Remember: Your core values are not set in stone. They may evolve over time as you learn and grow. The important thing is to be aware of your values and use them as a guiding force in your goal setting and decision-making.

Actionable Tip: Spend 15 minutes this week journaling about your core values. What are the top 3-5 values that are most important to you?

Values Clarification Exercise
Take some quiet time to reflect on your core values. Here are some prompts to guide you:

- **What are the most important qualities you admire in others?**
- **When have you felt most fulfilled in your life? What values were present in those situations?**
- **Imagine your ideal future self. What are the core principles that guide your life in this scenario?**
- **What are some non-negotiables for you in life? What are you unwilling to compromise on?**

"The only person you are destined to become is the person you decide to be."
- Ralph Waldo Emerson

By taking the time to identify your core values, you can set goals that resonate with your deepest desires and navigate the digital chaos with greater clarity and purpose.

Section 2

SMART Goals: Turning Dreams into Action

Have you ever set a New Year's resolution to "get healthy" or "be more productive," only to find yourself feeling discouraged and defeated by the end of the year? The problem may lie in the way you're setting your goals. Vague and unattainable aspirations are more likely to lead to frustration than achievement. This is where the SMART goal framework comes in – a powerful tool for setting clear, actionable goals that will propel you towards success.

What is SMART?
SMART is an acronym that stands for:

- **Specific:** Clearly define what you want to achieve. Instead of a vague goal like "improve my marketing," a specific goal might be "increase website traffic by 20% within the next quarter."

- **Measurable:** Establish a way to track your progress. How will you know if you've achieved your goal? Numbers are helpful, but other forms of measurement can be used as well. For example, a measurable goal for improving your public speaking skills might be to "deliver two presentations to local business groups by the end of the year."

- **Achievable:** Be realistic about what you can accomplish. While you should challenge yourself, your goals should also be attainable within a reasonable timeframe.

- **Relevant:** Ensure your goals align with your core values and overall objectives. A SMART goal should contribute to your bigger picture.

- **Time-Bound:** Set a deadline for achieving your goal. This creates a sense of urgency and helps you stay focused.

The Power of SMART Goals:
By setting SMART goals, you're more likely to achieve the following:

- **Increased Clarity:** The SMART framework forces you to define your goals precisely, leaving no room for ambiguity or procrastination.

- **Enhanced Motivation:** Measurable progress keeps you motivated and allows you to celebrate milestones along the way.

- **Improved Focus:** A clear deadline helps you prioritize tasks and stay on track.

- **Greater Sense of Accomplishment:** Achieving a well-defined goal is incredibly rewarding and fuels further success.

Write Down Your SMART Goals
Grab a pen and paper (or your favourite note-taking app) and use the SMART framework to write down your goals.

Here's an example to get you started:

Goal: Improve my public speaking skills (Not SMART)

SMART Goal: Deliver two presentations to local business groups by the end of the next quarter. I will rehearse each presentation in advance and time myself to ensure I stay within the allotted timeframe. I will also record myself practicing and actively seek feedback from a trusted colleague to identify areas for improvement. (This is a SMART Goal)

Actionable Tip: The SMART Goal Setting Process
This flowchart visually outlines the steps involved in creating effective and achievable goals using the SMART framework:

- **Step 1: Identify Your Desired Outcome.** What do you want to achieve? Be specific!

- **Step 2: Define Measurable Criteria.** How will you track your progress? Numbers are ideal, but other forms of measurement can be used as well.

- **Step 3: Set an Achievable Target.** Be ambitious, but realistic. Consider the resources and time available to you.

- **Step 4: Ensure Alignment with Values.** Does your goal support your core values and contribute to your bigger picture?

- **Step 5: Establish a Clear Deadline.** When do you want to achieve this goal? Having a deadline creates a sense of urgency and keeps you focused.

- **Step 6: Develop an Action Plan.** Break down your goal into smaller, actionable steps. What specific actions will you take to move closer to your goal?

Remember: Don't be afraid to adjust your goals as needed. As you learn and grow, your priorities may shift. The important thing is to have a clear roadmap to guide your journey and keep you moving forward.

"The best way to predict the future is to create it."
– Peter Drucker

By harnessing the power of SMART goals, you can transform your aspirations from vague wishes into actionable plans for success. This clarity and focus will empower you to conquer the digital chaos and achieve your goals in a meaningful and fulfilling way.

Section -3

Prioritization Techniques: From To-Do Tsunami to Focused Flow

Ever feel like your to-do list resembles a tidal wave, threatening to engulf you with its sheer volume? You're not alone. Busy professionals are bombarded with tasks, emails, and requests, making it difficult to know where to even begin. This is where prioritization techniques come in – powerful tools to help you sort through the chaos and focus on what truly matters.

The Eisenhower Matrix: A Simple Yet Powerful Tool

Imagine a two-by-two grid, with "Urgent" and "Not Urgent" on the x-axis, and "Important" and "Not Important" on the y-axis. This is the essence of the Eisenhower Matrix, a simple framework developed by Dwight D. Eisenhower, a US president who also served as a five-star general.

Here's how it works:

- **Urgent & Important:** These are the tasks that demand your immediate attention. Think looming deadlines, critical client meetings, or unexpected emergencies.

- **Not Urgent & Important:** Schedule time for these important, but not urgent tasks. This might include strategic planning, professional development, or relationship building activities. By scheduling them in advance, you ensure they don't get overshadowed by urgent tasks.

- **Urgent & Not Important:** These are often interruptions or distractions that can derail your focus. Delegate these tasks whenever possible, or politely decline if they don't contribute to your overall goals.

- **Not Urgent & Not Important:** Eliminate these tasks completely. They are the time-wasters and energy-drainers that can be safely removed from your to-do list.

Actionable Tip: Take sometime this week to categorize all your tasks within the matrix. This will give you a clear picture of what needs your immediate attention, what can be scheduled for later, and what can be eliminated altogether.

Beyond the Eisenhower Matrix:
The Eisenhower Matrix is a great starting point, but there are other prioritization techniques you can explore:

- **The ABC Method:** Classify tasks as A (high priority), B (medium priority), or C (low priority) based on their importance and impact.

- **The Time Blocking Method:** Schedule specific blocks of time in your calendar for focused work on high-priority tasks.

Remember: The key to effective prioritization is to find a system that works for you. Experiment with different techniques and find what helps you achieve the most important tasks while minimizing distractions and overwhelm.

Schedule Time for Your Most Important Tasks
Once you've identified your most important tasks using a prioritization technique like the Eisenhower Matrix, schedule dedicated time blocks in your calendar to focus on completing them. This will help you avoid multitasking and ensure you give these critical tasks the attention they deserve.

"What matters is not what you accomplish once, but what you keep up day by day."

– Marian Wright Edelman

By mastering the art of prioritization, you can transform your to-do list from a chaotic tsunami into a manageable stream, allowing you to focus on the tasks that truly move the needle towards your goals and reduce the digital clutter that can cloud your workday.

A Case Study:
Sarah, a passionate entrepreneur and owner of a thriving bakery, found herself drowning in a sea of details. Managing inventory, overseeing staff, handling social media, and brainstorming new recipe ideas left her feeling overwhelmed and stretched thin. She constantly felt like she was putting out fires instead of focusing on strategic growth.

A Values-Driven Approach:
Sarah decided to take a step back and re-evaluate her priorities. Through a values clarification exercise, she identified her core values: creativity and innovation. She realized that getting bogged down in administrative tasks was stifling her creative spirit and hindering her ability to develop innovative new products.

Setting SMART Goals:
With her core values in mind, Sarah set SMART goals to regain control. One of her goals was to "delegate 70% of daily administrative tasks to a virtual assistant within the next month." This ensured she had more time to focus on her passion – developing unique and delicious pastries for her customers.

Taking Action:
Sarah hired a virtual assistant to handle tasks like scheduling appointments, managing social media calendars, and processing invoices. This freed up her time to experiment with new recipes, brainstorm marketing campaigns, and meet with potential vendors. By delegating and prioritizing tasks that aligned with her core values, Sarah was able to reignite her passion and propel her bakery towards even greater success.

The Takeaway:

Sarah's story illustrates the power of prioritization. By identifying your core values and setting SMART goals that support them, you can delegate tasks that drain your energy and focus on the work that truly matters. This allows you to achieve a greater sense of purpose and fulfilment while propelling your business (or career) forward.

This case study demonstrates how prioritizing tasks based on their value alignment can lead to increased efficiency, reduced stress, and a renewed sense of purpose.

Chapter 5

Mastering Your Time Management: Tools and Techniques for Efficiency

Feeling like there just aren't enough hours in the day? You're not alone. Busy professionals are constantly bombarded with tasks, emails, and requests. It's easy to get overwhelmed and struggle to find focus. But what if there were ways to take control of your time and become a productivity powerhouse?

This chapter dives deep into the world of time management, equipping you with the tools and techniques to streamline your workday and achieve more in less time. We'll explore the power of scheduling, discover techniques like the Pomodoro Technique and timeboxing, and learn the art of saying no – a crucial skill for busy professionals.

By the end of this chapter, you'll have a toolkit filled with actionable strategies to:
- Craft a realistic and flexible schedule that keeps you focused.
- Conquer distractions and optimize your workflow.
- Prioritize ruthlessly and tackle your most important tasks first.
- Set boundaries and politely decline requests that overload your plate.

Imagine a workday where you feel in control, focused, and empowered. With the time management techniques in this chapter, that reality is within reach. Let's get started!

Section 1

The Power of Scheduling: Taming the Time Tiger

Ever feel like time is a ferocious tiger, constantly nipping at your heels and threatening to devour your entire to-do list? You're not alone. Busy professionals often struggle with a constant sense of urgency, flitting from task to task without ever feeling truly in control. This is where the power of scheduling comes in – your secret weapon for transforming that ferocious time tiger into a purring kitten, content to nap peacefully while you achieve your goals.

Why is Scheduling Important?
Imagine walking into a grocery store without a list. You wander aimlessly down aisles, grabbing random items that may or may not be what you need. This is essentially what happens when you approach your workday without a schedule. You get bombarded by emails, pulled in different directions by colleagues, and end up feeling scattered and unproductive.

Creating a Realistic and Flexible Schedule
The key to effective scheduling is striking a balance between structure and flexibility. Here's what you need to consider:

- **Identify Your Peak Productivity Times:** When are you naturally most focused and energized? Schedule deep work sessions for these times and lighter tasks for periods when your energy dips.

- **Block Out Focused Work Sessions:** Schedule specific time slots in your calendar dedicated to tackling high-priority tasks. This helps minimize distractions and keeps you on track.

- **Leave Room for Flexibility:** Unexpected events are inevitable. Build in buffer time throughout your day to handle interruptions without derailing your entire schedule.

- **Prioritize ruthlessly:** Use a prioritization technique like the Eisenhower Matrix (mentioned earlier) to identify the most important tasks that deserve a dedicated spot in your schedule.

Actionable Tip: Use daily or weekly schedule template. Fill it in with your tasks, meetings, and buffer times. This visual representation of your day will help you stay focused and ensure you're allocating time to the things that truly matter.

The Power of "No"
Even the most meticulously crafted schedule can fall apart if you can't say no to additional requests. Remember, it's okay to politely decline tasks that would overload your plate. By setting boundaries and protecting your schedule, you ensure you have the time and energy to focus on what truly matters.

"Time is not a renewable resource. Therefore, wasting it is the same as destroying it."
- Josh Billings

By harnessing the power of scheduling and mastering the art of saying no, you can transform your workday from a chaotic whirlwind into a streamlined symphony of productivity. You'll regain control of your time, reduce stress, and achieve your goals with greater focus and efficiency.

Section 2

Time Management Techniques: Your Productivity Power Tools

We've talked about the importance of scheduling, but what about those times you're actually **in the trenches** tackling your to-do list? Fear not, busy professional! Here are some powerful techniques to optimize your workflow, conquer distractions, and get more done in less time:

- **The Pomodoro Technique:** Ever feel like you spend hours staring at your screen, accomplishing very little? Enter the Pomodoro Technique, your weapon against procrastination. Here's the drill: Set a timer for 25 minutes and focus solely on one task. When the timer rings, reward yourself with a short break (5 minutes). Repeat this cycle four times, then take a longer break (20-30 minutes). This technique promotes laser focus and helps you avoid mental fatigue.

- **Timeboxing:** Feeling overwhelmed by a long list of tasks? Timeboxing can be your savior. Allocate specific time slots in your calendar for each task. For example, block out an hour for writing a report, 30 minutes for responding to emails, and 45 minutes for brainstorming a marketing campaign. Sticking to these timeboxes keeps you on track and prevents you from getting bogged down in any one task.

- **Batching:** Do you find yourself constantly switching gears between different types of tasks? This context-switching can be a major productivity killer. Batching offers a solution. Group similar tasks together and tackle them in one go. For example, dedicate a specific time slot to responding to all your emails, another for making phone calls, and another for administrative tasks. This reduces mental jumping jacks and allows you to enter a focused flow state for each type of activity.

Actionable Tip: Experiment with these techniques! Some people thrive with the structured focus of the Pomodoro Technique, while others prefer the flexibility of timeboxing. The key is to find what works best for you and your unique work style.

Time Management Techniques: We've explored some powerful techniques to optimize your workflow, but there's a whole toolbox out there! Experiment with different approaches like the **Eisenhower Matrix**, which helps prioritize tasks based on urgency and importance, or the **Getting Things Done (GTD)** method, which offers a comprehensive system for managing to-do lists and projects. Ultimately, the key is to find what works best for you and your unique work style.

Real-Life Example: Sarah, a marketing manager, constantly felt scattered by her overflowing inbox and never-ending to-do list. By implementing timeboxing, she dedicated specific time slots for checking emails and responding to messages. She also started using the Pomodoro Technique for focused writing sessions, allowing her to complete her reports and marketing copy in a fraction of the time it previously took.

Remember: These techniques are tools, not rigid rules. Adapt them to your specific needs and preferences. The goal is to find a system that empowers you to work smarter, not harder, and achieve your goals with greater efficiency.

"The difference between successful people and others is not a lack of strength, not a lack of knowledge, but rather a lack of will."

- Vince Lombardi

By incorporating these time management techniques into your workday, you'll transform from a scattered multitasker into a focused productivity machine. You'll conquer distractions, optimize your workflow, and achieve more in less time, leaving you feeling empowered and in control.

Real-Life Example:
Angel, a project manager, used to feel constantly bombarded by emails and to-do lists. Her workday felt chaotic, and she struggled to make significant progress on any task. She'd spend hours checking her inbox, feeling pulled in different directions by urgent requests.

The Transformation:
Determined to regain control, Angel decided to experiment with time management techniques. She implemented **timeboxing** by dedicating specific slots in her calendar for checking emails (twice a day) and responding to messages. This eliminated the constant distraction of incoming emails and allowed her to focus on deep work during the rest of her day.

She also adopted the **Pomodoro Technique**. By setting 25-minute timers for focused work sessions followed by short breaks, Angel improved her concentration and avoided mental fatigue. This approach allowed her to tackle complex tasks more efficiently and meet deadlines with greater ease.

The Result:
By incorporating timeboxing and the Pomodoro Technique, Angel transformed her workday. She felt calmer and more in control. Her focus improved, and she started making significant progress on her projects. The constant feeling of being overwhelmed became a thing of the past, replaced by a sense of accomplishment and productivity.

This example highlights the practical benefits of time management techniques, making them relatable and encouraging for readers facing similar challenges.

Section 3

The Art of Saying No:
Taking Back Control of Your Time

We've all been there: overflowing inboxes, endless requests, and that constant feeling of being stretched too thin. But what if there was a magic word to help you reclaim control of your schedule? Well, there is – it's **"no"**.

Saying no might feel uncomfortable at first, but it's a crucial skill for busy professionals. Here are some tips for setting boundaries and politely declining requests that would overload your plate:

- **Be Clear and Upfront:** A simple "no, thank you" is perfectly acceptable. You don't need to go into elaborate explanations.

- **Offer an Alternative:** If you can't take on a new task entirely, see if there's a smaller part you can contribute or suggest someone else who might be a better fit.

- **Explain Your Priorities:** Briefly explain that your schedule is already full with important projects. This helps the other person understand why you can't take on more.

- **Focus on "I" Statements:** Phrases like "I'm already swamped with deadlines" or "I wouldn't be able to give this the attention it deserves right now" are a respectful way to decline.

Real-Life Example: Anup, a software developer, constantly felt pulled in different directions by colleagues needing his help. He started politely saying no to requests that weren't urgent or didn't align with his current projects. By setting these boundaries, Anup regained control of his workload and was able to focus on delivering high-quality work on time.

Remember: Saying no isn't selfish, it's self-care. By protecting your time, you ensure you have the energy and focus to tackle your most important tasks and avoid burnout.

"Your time is your life. Don't waste it living someone else's dream."
                                                              - Steve Jobs

By mastering the art of saying no, you'll transform from a constantly overloaded worker into a focused professional. You'll reclaim control of your schedule, prioritize your well-being, and achieve your goals with renewed clarity and confidence.

Actionable Tips:
- **Experiment with different time management techniques to find what works best for you.** There are many approaches out there, like the Pomodoro Technique (discussed earlier) or the Eisenhower Matrix for prioritizing tasks. Try them out and see what helps you stay focused and productive.

- **Block out focused work sessions in your calendar and stick to them.** Treat these sessions like sacred appointments. Silence notifications, close distracting tabs, and let colleagues know you're unavailable. This dedicated time allows you to make significant progress on deep work tasks without interruptions.

customizable daily or weekly schedule template

This table provides a sample daily schedule with fictional times. You can customize it to fit your needs by adjusting the activities and time slots.

Time	Activity	Focus
7:00 AM - 8:00 AM	Wake Up, Exercise, Shower, Breakfast	Personal Wellbeing & Routines
8:00 AM - 9:30 AM	Focused Work Session 1 (Write Marketing Report)	High-Priority Project/Task
9:30 AM - 10:00 AM	Check Emails & Respond (Batch similar tasks)	Communication & Organization

Time	Activity	Focus
10:00 AM - 10:30 AM	Team Meeting (Discuss Upcoming Project Launch)	Teamwork & Project Progress
10:30 AM - 11:30 AM	Lunch Break	Rest & Refuel
11:30 AM - 1:00 PM	Focused Work Session 2 (Develop Social Media Campaign)	High-Priority Project/Task
1:00 PM - 1:30 PM	Administrative Tasks (Update Client Records)	Clearing the To-Do List
1:30 PM - 2:00 PM	Learning & Development (Watch Online Course on Project Management)	Professional Growth & Upskilling
2:00 PM - 2:30 PM	Review & Plan (Review accomplishments, set goals for tomorrow)	Reflection & Planning
2:30 PM - 5:00 PM	Wrap Up & Downtime (Read a book, go for a walk)	Personal Wellbeing & Recharge

Note: This is just a sample schedule. Feel free to adjust it based on your workday and preferences.

Additional Tips:
- Include buffer time throughout your day for unexpected tasks or interruptions.
- Take breaks throughout the day to avoid burnout.
- Schedule time for personal errands or appointments if needed.
- Review and adjust your schedule as needed throughout the week.

Practice assertive communication to politely decline requests that don't align with your priorities. It's okay to say no! A simple "Thank you, but I'm already swamped with deadlines right now" works wonders. You can also offer an alternative or suggest someone else who might be a better fit for the task.

Chapter 6

Optimizing Your Digital Workspace: Tools for Focus and Flow

Welcome to Chapter 6: Optimizing Your Digital Workspace: Tools for Focus and Flow!

Feeling overwhelmed by the constant digital clutter clogging your computer and phone? You're not alone. In today's fast-paced world, our digital spaces often become overflowing with emails, unread articles, and unused apps. This clutter can be a major drain on our focus and productivity, leaving us feeling stressed and behind.

But fear not! Just like a messy desk hinders efficiency, a cluttered digital workspace can be tamed. This chapter equips you with the tools and techniques to transform your digital environment into a haven of productivity.

We'll embark on a three-pronged approach:

- **Digital Decluttering:** Learn strategies to streamline your digital life, including organizing files, unsubscribing from unnecessary emails, and deleting unused apps. Imagine the satisfaction of finding any document in seconds with a clean and organized digital filing system!

- **Harnessing Technology for Good:** Discover the power of technology to work for you! We'll explore productivity apps, project management tools, and automation software that can streamline your workflow and free up your time for the things that truly matter. Think of it as building your own team of "tech superheroes" to boost your productivity.

- **Creating a Distraction-Free Environment:** We've tackled the clutter and introduced your tech allies, but what about those pesky distractions constantly hijacking your focus? Here, you'll learn how to silence notification monsters, minimize distractions on your devices, and create a dedicated workspace for optimal focus.

Throughout the chapter, we'll provide actionable tips you can implement immediately, along with real-life examples to illustrate the effectiveness of these strategies.

Get ready to reclaim control of your digital life, unlock a new level of focus, and experience the joy of a truly optimized digital workspace! Let's dive in.

Section 1

Digital Decluttering: Tame the Tech Tsunami

Feeling overwhelmed by the constant barrage of emails, notifications, and unread articles clogging your digital space? You're not alone! Busy professionals like us often find themselves drowning in a sea of digital clutter. This can lead to wasted time, decreased focus, and a constant feeling of being behind.

But fear not! Just like a messy desk can hinder productivity, a cluttered digital workspace can be a major drain on your energy and focus. The good news is, with a few simple strategies, you can tame the tech tsunami and reclaim control of your digital life.

Here are some actionable steps to get you started:

- **Organize Your Files:** Imagine rummaging through a drawer overflowing with papers. It's frustrating, right? The same goes for your digital files. Take some time to create folders and subfolders to categorize your documents, photos, and downloads. This will make it easier to find what you need when you need it, saving you precious time and frustration.

- **Unsubscribe from Unnecessary Emails:** Does your inbox resemble a never-ending black hole of promotional emails and forgotten newsletters? Unsubscribe ruthlessly! Take control of your inbox by unsubscribing from emails you don't read or find valuable. This will reduce clutter and prevent distractions that can derail your focus.

- **Delete Unused Apps:** How many apps lurk on your phone or computer, forgotten and unused? Regularly audit your apps and delete the ones you don't use anymore. Not only will this free up valuable storage space, but it will also minimize the temptation to mindlessly scroll through social media or check news updates.

Actionable Tip:

Utilize file management systems to organize your digital documents and folders. (Benefit: Spend less time searching for files and boost your productivity by knowing exactly where everything is located.)

- Create folders with clear and descriptive names for different categories of documents (e.g., "Project Reports," "Client Invoices," "Personal Documents").

- Use subfolders for further organization within each category.
- Regularly review and clean up your folders to maintain a clutter-free digital filing system.

Unsubscribe from unwanted emails and notifications to reduce clutter. (Benefit: Minimize distractions and regain control of your inbox. A clean inbox promotes a sense of calm and allows you to focus on important messages.)

- Unsubscribe from promotional emails and newsletters you don't read or find valuable.

- Utilize "unsubscribe" buttons found within email content or manage your preferences on company websites.

- Consider creating filters to automatically categorize or delete low-priority emails.

By implementing these simple digital decluttering strategies, you'll be well on your way to a calmer, more organized digital workspace. This, in turn, will set you up for improved focus, increased productivity, and a newfound sense of control over your digital life. Remember, a clutter-free digital space leads to a clutter-free mind!

Section 2

Harnessing Technology for Good: Your Digital Ally

We've tackled digital decluttering, and now it's time to unleash the power of technology to work for you! Imagine a world where apps magically organize your tasks, software helps you manage complex projects, and repetitive work gets done automatically. Well, guess what? That world exists! There's a whole arsenal of productivity tools waiting to streamline your workflow and free up your time for the things that truly matter.

Let's explore some tech superheroes ready to join your productivity team:

- **Task Managers:** Feeling overwhelmed by to-do lists? Task managers like Todoist or Asana can be your lifesavers. These apps help you create, organize, and prioritize tasks, ensuring you never miss a deadline and always know what needs to be done next.

- **Time Trackers:** Ever wonder where your day goes? Time trackers like Toggl or RescueTime shed light on how you actually spend your time. This self-awareness is key to identifying areas for improvement and optimizing your schedule for maximum productivity.

- **Calendar Tools:** Juggling meetings, deadlines, and appointments can feel like a high-wire act. Calendar tools like Google Calendar or Outlook Calendar come to the rescue. Use them to schedule your entire day, set reminders, and collaborate with colleagues – all in one place.

- **Project Management Tools:** Managing complex projects requires organization and collaboration. Project management tools like Trello or Asana can be your secret weapon. These platforms help you visualize tasks, track progress, and ensure everyone on the team is on the same page.

- **Automation Software:** Feeling bogged down by repetitive tasks? Automation software like Zapier or IFTTT can be your game-changer. Automate tasks like sending follow-up emails, scheduling social media posts, or copying data between applications. This frees up your valuable time and mental energy for more strategic work.

Actionable Tip: Not sure which tools are right for you? Many offers free trials or basic versions, so you can experiment and find the perfect fit.

Explore productivity apps like task managers, time trackers, and calendar tools. (Benefit: Streamline your workflow by leveraging technology to manage your tasks, track your time, and schedule your day effectively.)

- Task managers (e.g., Todoist, Asana) help you create, organize, and prioritize tasks, ensuring you never miss a deadline and always know what needs to be done next.

- Time trackers (e.g., Toggl, RescueTime) shed light on how you actually spend your time, helping you identify areas for improvement and optimize your schedule.

- Calendar tools (e.g., Google Calendar, Outlook Calendar) allow you to schedule your entire day, set reminders, and collaborate with colleagues – all in one place.

Utilize automation tools for repetitive tasks like data entry or social media posting. (Benefit: Free up your valuable time and mental energy for more strategic work by automating tedious and repetitive tasks.)

- Explore automation software (e.g., Zapier, IFTTT) to automate tasks like sending follow-up emails, scheduling social media posts, or copying data between applications.

By harnessing the power of these productivity tools, you can transform your digital workspace into a well-oiled machine. Imagine the feeling of accomplishment as you breeze through your to-do list, meet deadlines with ease, and finally feel in control of your ever-growing workload. Technology can be your biggest ally in the fight against digital overwhelm, so don't be afraid to explore and leverage its power!

Section 3

Creating a Distraction-Free Environment: Tame the Notification Monster

We've decluttered your digital space and equipped you with productivity tools. Now, let's tackle those pesky distractions that keep hijacking your focus. Let's face it, between email notifications, social media pings, and the allure of news alerts, our devices can be real attention vampires! But fear not, with a few tweaks, you can transform your digital environment into a haven of focus and productivity.

Here are some actionable tips to silence the notification monster and reclaim your concentration:

- **Silence Notifications:** Constant notifications are productivity killers. Take control! Silence unnecessary notifications on your computer and phone. This might sound drastic, but trust us, you won't miss the constant barrage of pings and dings. Most apps and programs allow you to customize notifications, so silence the ones that disrupt your workflow and keep the truly important ones.

- **Utilize Focus Modes:** Many devices offer built-in "focus modes" or "do not disturb" features. These settings temporarily silence notifications and can be a lifesaver during deep work sessions or important meetings. Activate them when you need uninterrupted focus and reclaim your attention space.

- **Browser Extensions for Distraction Control:** Feeling tempted to disappear down a social media rabbit hole during work hours? There are browser extensions available that can block distracting websites for set periods. These can be a powerful tool for staying on track and avoiding procrastination.

- **Create a Dedicated Workspace:** If possible, designate a specific area in your home or office as your workspace. This physical separation can help prime your mind for focus. Avoid working from your bed or couch, as these environments are typically associated with relaxation and can blur the lines between work and personal time.

Actionable Tip: Experiment and find what works for you! Some people thrive in complete silence, while others prefer background music. Play around with different settings and create a focus environment that keeps you engaged and productive.

Set up focus modes on your devices to minimize notifications and distractions. (**Benefit:** Enhance your focus and achieve laser-sharp concentration by silencing the notification monster.)

- Many devices offer built-in "focus modes" or "do not disturb" features. Activate them when you need uninterrupted focus and reclaim your attention space.

- Consider customizing notification settings on individual apps and programs to silence the ones that disrupt your workflow.

By implementing these strategies, you can create a distraction-free zone that empowers you to achieve laser focus and conquer your workday. Remember, a little effort goes a long way in silencing the digital noise and reclaiming control of your attention.

Real-Life Example: Conquering Distractions for Academic Success

Ever feel like your phone is the enemy of productivity? Clara, a college student constantly bombarded by social media notifications, could definitely relate. Studying for exams felt like an uphill battle against the constant buzz and ping of her phone. Glancing at a quick notification inevitably led to a scroll through her feed, eating away at precious study time and leaving her feeling frustrated and behind.

Determined to improve her focus, Clara decided to take action. She implemented two key strategies:

- **Time Blocking:** Clara downloaded a time management app and used the "time blocking" feature to schedule dedicated study sessions. During these blocks, she silenced her phone notifications and even used a website blocker to restrict access to distracting social media platforms. This allowed her to concentrate solely on the task at hand, maximizing her study time and minimizing distractions.

- **Focus Environment:** Clara also created a dedicated study space in her room. This area was free from clutter and distractions, promoting a sense of calm and focus. Having a designated space for studying helped her mentally transition into work mode and avoid the temptation to multitask.

The results were impressive. By implementing these strategies, Sarah noticed a significant improvement in her focus and concentration. She was able to absorb information more effectively, complete her assignments on time, and ultimately achieved better grades. Clara's story is a powerful reminder that with a few tweaks to our digital environment, we can reclaim control of our attention and conquer distractions.

Chapter 7

Cultivating a Growth Mindset: Embracing Challenges for Long-Term Gains

Feeling overwhelmed by the ever-evolving digital world? Do technical glitches and project roadblocks leave you discouraged? If so, you're not alone. Busy professionals like us face a constant barrage of challenges in the digital age. But what if we told you there's a secret weapon to conquering these challenges and achieving long-term success?

That secret weapon is a concept called a **growth mindset**.

What is a Growth Mindset?
Imagine your brain is like a muscle. The more you exercise it, the stronger it gets. A growth mindset operates under this same principle. It's the belief that your intelligence, skills, and abilities can be developed through effort, learning, and perseverance. In other words, you're not stuck with a set amount of talent – you can always grow and improve!

Why is a Growth Mindset Important?
The opposite of a growth mindset is a fixed mindset. People with a fixed mindset believe their abilities are set in stone. This can be incredibly limiting, especially in the dynamic digital world. When faced with challenges, those with a fixed mindset often give up easily or avoid them altogether. On the other hand, a growth mindset empowers you to **see challenges as opportunities to learn and grow**. You embrace setbacks as temporary roadblocks and use them as stepping stones on your path to success.

The Benefits of a Growth Mindset:

Here are just a few reasons why cultivating a growth mindset is essential for thriving in the digital age:

- **Increased Resilience:** When you believe you can learn and improve, you're better equipped to bounce back from setbacks. You see failures as opportunities to learn and grow stronger.
- **Enhanced Motivation:** A growth mindset fuels your motivation. Knowing you can develop your skills keeps you pushing forward, even when things get tough.
- **Lifelong Learning:** The digital world is constantly changing. A growth mindset fosters a love of learning, which is crucial for adapting to new technologies and staying ahead of the curve.

Characteristic	Growth Mindset	Fixed Mindset
Belief System	Intelligence and abilities can be developed through effort and learning.	Intelligence and abilities are fixed traits.
Approach to Challenges	Sees challenges as opportunities to learn and grow.	Avoids challenges or gives up easily.
View of Effort	Views effort as a path to mastery.	Views effort as pointless if you're not naturally talented.
View of Setbacks	Sees setbacks as temporary and a chance to improve.	Sees setbacks as proof of failure.

By embracing a growth mindset, you'll unlock your full potential and transform the way you approach challenges in the digital world. This chapter will equip you with the tools and strategies to cultivate a growth mindset and set yourself up for long-term success.

Remember: We all have a mix of both mindsets. The key is to be aware of your negative self-talk and challenge those fixed mindset beliefs. With consistent effort and practice, you can develop a growth mindset and unlock a world of possibilities in the digital age!

Section 1

The Power of Positive Thinking:
Flip the Script on Your Inner Critic

Ever feel like your inner voice is your worst enemy? You're not alone. Busy professionals like us often face a constant barrage of negative self-talk, especially when dealing with challenges or setbacks. Phrases like "I can't do this" or "I'm not good enough" can quickly drain our motivation and leave us feeling overwhelmed.

But what if we told you there's a way to silence the inner critic and unlock your full potential? That's where the power of positive thinking comes in!

Here's the deal: Our thoughts have a significant impact on our actions and ultimately, our results. By developing a more positive and solution-oriented mindset, we can approach challenges with a sense of empowerment rather than dread. This shift in perspective can lead to several benefits:

- **Increased Resilience:** When faced with setbacks, a positive mindset allows you to bounce back quicker and learn from your mistakes. You see failures not as roadblocks, but as stepping stones on your path to success.

- **Enhanced Motivation:** A positive outlook fuels your motivation. Believing in your ability to learn and grow keeps you pushing forward, even when things get tough.

- **Improved Problem-Solving:** A positive mind is a creative mind. When you approach challenges with an open mind and a "can-do" attitude, you're more likely to find creative solutions and overcome obstacles.

Actionable Tip: Trade Self-Doubt for Daily Affirmations:
We all have moments of self-doubt. But instead of dwelling on negative thoughts, try replacing them with positive affirmations. These are short, powerful statements that reinforce your belief in yourself and your abilities.
Here are some examples to get you started:

- "I am capable and confident."
- "I learn from my mistakes and grow stronger."
- "I am worthy of success."

Repeating these affirmations daily can help combat negative self-talk and boost your confidence in the face of challenges.

Now that you understand the power of a growth mindset, let's dive into some actionable tips to help you cultivate it in your daily life.

Challenge Negative Self-Talk with Daily Affirmations: Our inner voice can be our worst critic. But here's the good news: you can silence the negativity with daily affirmations! These are short, powerful statements that reinforce your belief in yourself and your abilities.

Here's how to do it:
- **Start small:** Choose 1-2 affirmations that resonate with you.
- **Repeat daily:** Say your affirmations out loud or write them down first thing in the morning or before tackling a challenging task.
- **Examples of affirmations:** "I am capable and confident." "I learn from my mistakes and grow stronger." "I am worthy of success."

By repeating these affirmations daily, you'll gradually chip away at negative self-talk and replace it with empowering beliefs.

Remember: Cultivating a positive mindset is a journey, not a destination. There will be days when negative thoughts creep back in. But with consistent effort and practice, you can develop the power of positive thinking and transform your approach to challenges, ultimately unlocking your full potential for success.

From Rejection to Results: Jenny's Sales Success Story
Jenny had always been a high performer. A natural communicator, she landed a coveted sales position at a tech startup. But the initial excitement soon gave way to discouragement. Rejection after rejection chipped away at her confidence. "Maybe I'm not cut out for sales," she thought, her fixed mindset taking hold.

One day, during a team meeting, Jenny's manager, a seasoned sales veteran named Michael, noticed her slump. He pulled her aside and shared his secret weapon: a **growth mindset**. He explained how viewing challenges as learning opportunities could transform her approach to rejection.

Intrigued, Jenny decided to give it a try. Instead of dwelling on the "no," she started asking for feedback after each rejection. She learned to identify areas where she could improve her pitch, refine her product knowledge, and tailor her approach to different customer needs.

This shift in perspective was a game-changer. Jenny's positive attitude and willingness to learn excelled through during her interactions. She became more confident in her abilities and passionate about the product she was selling. The rejections, once roadblocks, became stepping stones on her path to success.

Within a few months, Jenny's results started to soar. Her positive attitude and focus on continuous improvement resonated with clients. She consistently exceeded her sales targets and became a top performer in the company. Jenny's story is a powerful testament to the transformative power of a growth mindset. By adopting this approach, she not only overcame challenges but thrived in a demanding sales environment.

Actionable Tip: The "Ups and Downs" Journal:
Here's a simple trick to develop resilience: keep an "Ups and Downs" journal. Each day, jot down a challenge you faced and how you overcame it. Reviewing these entries will remind you of your past successes and boost your confidence when facing future hurdles.

Developing Resilience: Bounce Back Like a Boss

Let's face it, setbacks are inevitable in the digital world. Maybe you lose an important document, miss a deadline due to a tech glitch, or experience a frustrating online meeting filled with connection issues. These moments can be discouraging, but here's the good news: **developing resilience** is a superpower you can cultivate!

Resilience is all about your ability to bounce back from challenges and learn from your mistakes. It's about picking yourself up, dusting yourself off, and coming back stronger than ever. Here are some tips to help you become a resilience rockstar:

1. Reframe Your Thinking: Instead of dwelling on the negativity of a setback, try to see it as a learning opportunity. Ask yourself: "What can I learn from this experience?" "How can I prevent this from happening again?" By focusing on the lessons learned, you'll be better equipped to navigate similar situations in the future.

2. Analyze the Cause: Take some time to identify what went wrong. Was it a technical issue? Did you miss a step in your process? Understanding the root cause of the setback can help you develop strategies to avoid it next time.

3. Embrace Experimentation: Don't be afraid to try new things! Sometimes, the best way to overcome a setback is to experiment with different approaches. See this as an opportunity to find a better, more efficient way to get things done.

4. Celebrate Small Victories: Building resilience isn't about avoiding mistakes altogether. It's about celebrating your progress, no matter how small. Did you finally fix that buggy spreadsheet? Did you figure out a new way to organize your files? Acknowledge these small wins – they're stepping stones on your path to mastering the digital world!

Remember, setbacks are a normal part of the digital journey. By developing resilience, you can transform them into valuable learning experiences and propel yourself towards achieving your goals!

Section 3

Celebrating Small Wins: High Fives for Tiny Victories

We all love the feeling of accomplishing a major goal, that celebratory fist pump after a successful presentation or the sigh of relief after finally conquering a complex project. But what about the smaller victories? The ones that might seem insignificant in the grand scheme of things?

Here's the truth: **celebrating small wins is just as important** (if not more!) than the big ones. Why? Because acknowledging your progress, no matter how small, fuels your motivation and keeps you moving forward, especially in the digital world where challenges can pop up like pesky browser notifications.

Here's the science behind it: When you celebrate a win, big or small, your brain releases a dose of dopamine, the "feel-good" neurotransmitter. This dopamine rush motivates you to keep striving and achieving. Think of it like giving yourself a high five for a job well done!

Here are some reasons why celebrating small wins is a total game-changer:

- **Boosts Motivation:** Acknowledging your progress, no matter how small, gives you a sense of accomplishment. These feeling fuels your motivation and keeps you pushing forward, even when faced with larger challenges.

- **Increases Confidence:** Celebrating your wins reinforces your belief in your abilities. Over time, this can lead to increased confidence and a can-do attitude, which is crucial for navigating the ever-changing digital landscape.

- **Keeps You on Track:** The digital world can be full of distractions. Celebrating your small wins helps you stay focused on your goals and prevents you from getting discouraged by setbacks.

Actionable Tip: The "Victory Dance" (Optional, but Fun!)
Feeling overwhelmed by your to-do list? Here's a fun way to celebrate small wins: have a "victory dance" every time you complete a task. It doesn't have to be elaborate – a quick air guitar solo or a silly jig will do the trick! This playful approach will boost your mood and keep you motivated to tackle the next item on your list.

Track Your Progress and Celebrate Milestones:
Staying motivated is key to cultivating a growth mindset. A great way to do this is to **track your progress and celebrate your milestones**.

Here's how to do it:
- **Set goals:** Break down your digital goals into smaller, achievable steps.

- **Track your progress:** Use a progress tracker or journal to monitor your accomplishments, no matter how small.

- **Celebrate your wins:** Take the time to acknowledge your achievements, big or small. This reinforces your sense of accomplishment and keeps you motivated.

- **Example:** Did you finally conquer your overflowing inbox? Celebrate by treating yourself to a coffee break!

By tracking your progress and celebrating your milestones, you'll stay motivated on your journey towards digital mastery.

Remember: Every accomplishment, big or small, is a step in the right direction. So, don't shy away from celebrating your victories, no matter how tiny they may seem. By taking the time to acknowledge your progress, you'll be fuelling your motivation and setting yourself up for long-term success in the digital world!

Chapter 8

Implementing Healthy Habits for Peak Performance

Welcome to Chapter 8! In today's fast-paced world, staying focused and productive can feel like an uphill battle. We juggle constant digital demands, long to-do lists, and often neglect the very things that fuel our well-being – sleep, nutrition, and exercise. But here's the good news: these aren't just lifestyle choices; they're the cornerstones of peak performance.

This chapter delves into the science-backed connection between healthy habits and a sharper, more energized you. We'll explore three key pillars:

- **Sleep: The Recharge Button for Your Brain:** Discover how prioritizing quality sleep isn't just about feeling well-rested; it's crucial for optimal cognitive function. Learn how sleep helps solidify memories, enhance creativity, and sharpen your focus. Imagine your brain as a high-performance computer – sleep is the essential downtime for processing information and running at peak speeds.

- **Fuelling Your Focus: Brainpower on a Plate:** We are what we eat! Explore the powerful link between nutrition and brain function. We'll debunk myths about "brain food" and guide you towards a balanced diet rich in brain-boosting nutrients. From colourful fruits and vegetables to healthy fats and lean protein, you'll discover how to nourish your brain for optimal performance.

- **Move Your Body, Boost Your Mind:** Sitting glued to your chair won't do your brain any favours. Exercise isn't just about physical fitness; it's a potent tool for enhancing brainpower. Discover how physical activity increases blood flow to the brain, improves cognitive function, and even combats stress. We'll provide actionable tips for busy professionals to integrate movement into their workday, even in short bursts.

Throughout the chapter, we'll share real-life examples of individuals who transformed their work lives by prioritizing healthy habits. You'll also find practical "Actionable Tips" to help you implement these strategies – visualize your success with the **Productivity Pyramid**, learn how to establish a sleep hygiene routine, and discover tips for incorporating brain-boosting foods and movement into your busy schedule.

By the end of this chapter, you'll be equipped with the knowledge and tools to build a foundation for peak performance. Remember, a healthy and energized you is a more productive and successful you. Let's dive in and unlock your full potential!

Section 1

The Importance of Sleep:
Recharge Your Brain for Peak Performance

Ever feel like your brain is running on fumes? You struggle to focus, forget important details, and by lunchtime, you're already dragging yourself through the day. Sound familiar? If so, you're not alone. Many busy professionals fall into the trap of skimping on sleep, sacrificing precious rest for that extra hour of work. But here's the thing: skimping on sleep backfires in the long run.

Science shows that sleep isn't just about feeling well-rested; it's crucial for our brains to function at their peak. While we snooze, our brains are busy consolidating memories, flushing out toxins, and rewiring neural pathways. This translates to **sharper focus, improved problem-solving skills, and enhanced creativity**. Basically, sleep is like hitting the "restart" button on your brain, leaving you feeling refreshed and ready to tackle whatever the day throws your way.

Think of your brain like a high-performance computer. Just like any computer, it needs regular downtime to process information, clear its cache, and run at optimal speeds. When you prioritize sleep, you're giving your brain the rest it needs to perform at its best. This translates to **increased productivity, better decision-making, and a sharper memory**.

So, the next time you're tempted to burn the midnight oil, remember: a good night's sleep is an investment in your productivity and well-being. In the next section, we'll explore some actionable tips to help you develop a sleep routine that will leave you feeling recharged and ready to conquer your digital world!

Nutrition for the Brain: Feed Your Focus
Ever feel like your brain hits a mid-afternoon slump? You reach for that third cup of coffee, but it only provides a temporary jolt. The truth is, what you eat plays a major role in how well your brain functions. Think of your brain as a

high-powered computer – it needs the right fuel to perform at its best.

So, what kind of fuel are we talking about? Here's the good news: you don't need fancy supplements or expensive "brain food" products. The key is to focus on a **balanced diet** rich in the following brain-boosting nutrients:

- **Fruits and Vegetables:** Packed with antioxidants and vitamins, these colorful powerhouses help protect your brain cells and improve cognitive function.

- **Whole Grains:** Whole grains provide a sustained source of energy, keeping your brain focused and alert throughout the day. Think whole-wheat bread, brown rice, and quinoa.

- **Healthy Fats:** Don't fear fat! Healthy fats, like those found in fatty fish, avocado, and nuts, are essential for building brain cells and improving memory.

- **Lean Protein:** Protein is the building block for all cells, including brain cells. Lean protein sources like chicken, fish, and beans help keep you feeling full and energized.

Actionable Tips:
- **Plan your meals:** Avoid unhealthy vending machine options by prepping healthy snacks and lunches in advance.

- **Pack a colourful lunch box:** Fill your lunch with a variety of fruits and veggies for a brainpower boost.

- **Start your day with breakfast:** Don't skip breakfast! A healthy breakfast kickstarts your metabolism and helps you stay focused throughout the morning.

- **Hydration is key:** Drinking plenty of water throughout the day keeps your brain functioning optimally. Dehydration can lead to fatigue and decreased focus.

Real-Life Example:
Sarathi, a talented programmer, used to pride himself on his ability to work long hours. Fuelled by sugary drinks and instant ramen, he'd often pull all-nighters to meet deadlines. However, this lifestyle started taking its toll. Sarathi constantly felt tired, his focus was shot, and even simple tasks seemed like an uphill battle. Bugs in his code became more frequent, and his productivity plummeted.

One particularly frustrating day, after spending hours debugging a seemingly simple issue, Sarathi knew something had to change. He stumbled upon an article about the importance of sleep for cognitive function. Intrigued, he started researching the connection between sleep hygiene, nutrition, and brainpower. What he discovered was a revelation.

Sarathi decided to take action. He swapped late-night coding sessions for a consistent sleep schedule, prioritizing a relaxing bedtime routine. He traded sugary drinks for water and stocked his pantry with brain-boosting foods like fruits, vegetables, and whole grains. He even started incorporating short walks into his workday to get his blood pumping.

The changes weren't easy at first. Sarathi's body craved the sugar rush of his old habits. But slowly, he started noticing a difference. He woke up feeling refreshed and energized. His focus sharpened, and his brain seemed to work faster. He tackled complex coding problems with renewed clarity, and the bugs became less frequent. Most importantly, David rediscovered his passion for programming.

Sarathi's story is a testament to the power of prioritizing healthy habits. By taking care of his physical and mental well-being, he not only improved his overall health but also unlocked his full potential as a programmer. His journey serves as an inspiration for all busy professionals struggling with digital overwhelm. Remember, you are what you eat and how you sleep. By investing in yourself, you invest in your productivity and success.

Remember, you are what you eat! By nourishing your body with the right foods, you're giving your brain the fuel it needs to perform at its peak. In the next section, we'll explore the power of movement and how exercise can further enhance your brainpower and well-being.

Section 2

The Power of Movement:
Get Your Body Moving, Boost Your Brainpower

Feeling glued to your chair? You're not alone. Busy professionals often spend hours hunched over screens, neglecting the importance of physical activity. But here's the secret: exercise isn't just about physical fitness; it's a powerful tool for **boosting your brainpower**.

Think of it like this: when you exercise, your heart rate increases, pumping oxygen-rich blood to your brain. This oxygen rush fuels your brain cells, leading to several benefits:

- **Stress Reduction:** Exercise is a natural stress reliever. Physical activity triggers the release of endorphins, those feel-good chemicals that combat stress hormones and leave you feeling calmer and more focused.

- **Increased Energy Levels:** Regular exercise improves your cardiovascular health, giving you more stamina and endurance throughout the day. Say goodbye to afternoon slumps!

- **Improved Cognitive Function:** Studies show that exercise can enhance memory, sharpen focus, and even boost creativity. It's like a workout for your brain!

Actionable Tips:
- **Short bursts are better than none:** Don't have time for a long gym session? No problem! Even small bursts of activity can make a big difference. Take a brisk walk during your lunch break, do some squats while waiting for the coffee machine, or climb the stairs instead of taking the elevator.

- **Find an activity you enjoy:** Exercise shouldn't feel like a chore! Find an activity you genuinely enjoy, whether it's dancing, swimming, yoga, or a team sport. This will make you more likely to stick with it.

- **Make it a social activity:** Grab a colleague for a walk during your break or join a lunchtime fitness class. Having a workout buddy can keep you motivated and accountable.

Real-Life Example:
Manju, a graphic designer, used to feel constantly drained and overwhelmed by her workload. Sitting for long periods left her with back pain and a foggy mind. She decided to incorporate short walks into her workday. To her surprise, these short bursts of activity made a significant difference. Manju noticed she had more energy, improved focus, and even felt more creative during her design sessions.

Remember, even small changes can make a big impact. By incorporating regular physical activity into your routine, you'll not only feel better physically, but you'll also be giving your brain the boost it needs to perform at its peak.

Actionable Tips:
Imagine a pyramid. At the base of this pyramid lie three essential building blocks for peak performance: sleep, nutrition, and exercise. A strong foundation is crucial for a stable and productive you!

Sleep Hygiene:
Creating a relaxing bedtime routine can significantly improve your sleep quality. Here are some tips to get you started:

- **Set a consistent sleep schedule:** Go to bed and wake up at the same time each day, even on weekends. This helps regulate your body's natural sleep-wake cycle.

- **Power down before bed:** Avoid screens (phones, laptops, TVs) for at least an hour before bedtime. The blue light emitted from these devices can disrupt your sleep cycle.

- **Create a sleep sanctuary:** Make sure your bedroom is cool, dark, and quiet. Invest in blackout curtains and earplugs if necessary.

- **Wind down with relaxing activities:** Take a warm bath, read a book, or practice gentle yoga before bed. Avoid stimulating activities like work emails or watching TV.

Fuel Your Brain with Brainpower Food:
Nourishing your body with the right foods is essential for optimal brain function. Here are some simple tips to keep in mind:

- **Plan your meals:** Avoid unhealthy temptations by prepping healthy snacks and lunches in advance. Stock your pantry with brain-boosting ingredients like fruits, vegetables, whole grains, nuts, and lean protein sources.

- **Pack a colourful lunch box:** Fill your lunch with a variety of fruits and veggies for a midday energy boost and a dose of essential vitamins and antioxidants.

- **Start your day with breakfast:** Don't skip breakfast! A healthy breakfast kickstarts your metabolism and helps you stay focused and energized throughout the morning. Choose options like oatmeal with berries, whole-wheat toast with avocado, or a Greek yogurt parfait.

- **Stay hydrated:** Drinking plenty of water throughout the day is crucial for overall health and brain function. Dehydration can lead to fatigue and decreased focus. Aim for eight glasses of water daily.

Move Your Body, Boost Your Mind:
Exercise doesn't have to be a time commitment. Here are some tips to integrate physical activity into your busy schedule:
- **Short bursts are powerful:** Don't have time for a gym session? No worries! Take the stairs instead of the elevator, do some stretches or squats while waiting for your coffee, or park further away and walk to your destination.

- **Find activities you enjoy:** Exercise shouldn't feel like a chore! Explore different activities like dancing, swimming, yoga, team sports, or even brisk walking. Choose something you genuinely enjoy to increase your chances of sticking with it.

- **Make it social:** Grab a colleague for a walk during your break or join a lunchtime fitness class with friends. Having a workout buddy can keep you motivated and accountable.

Remember, consistency is key! By incorporating these actionable tips into your daily routine, you'll be well on your way to building a solid foundation for peak performance and a healthier, happier you.

Visualize Your Success: The Productivity Pyramid
Imagine this pyramid. At the base of this pyramid lie three essential building blocks for peak performance: sleep, nutrition, and exercise.

We've called this the **Productivity Pyramid**. Just like a real pyramid, if any of these foundational elements are weak, your entire structure becomes less stable. However, by prioritizing all three aspects, you can create a solid base for optimal brain function, sustained energy, and overall well-being.

By prioritizing these foundational elements and building a strong Productivity Pyramid, you'll be well on your way to unlocking your full potential and achieving peak performance in all areas of your life.

Chapter 9

Maintaining Motivation and Avoiding Burnout

Ever feel like you're constantly running on fumes? You drag yourself out of bed in the morning already exhausted, the never-ending to-do list hangs over your head like a dark cloud, and even small tasks feel like a monumental effort. Sound familiar? If so, you might be experiencing burnout.

Burnout isn't just about feeling tired. It's a state of emotional, physical, and mental exhaustion caused by prolonged or excessive stress. Think of it like your body and mind hitting the brakes because they've simply had enough. This chapter delves into the signs and symptoms of burnout, a critical first step in recognizing and addressing this issue.

We'll explore:

- **Constant Exhaustion:** Feeling drained all the time, even after a good night's sleep.

- **Cynicism and Detachment:** Losing enthusiasm for your work and colleagues, and feeling emotionally distant.

- **Reduced Productivity:** A noticeable decline in performance, making careless mistakes and struggling to meet deadlines.

But burnout isn't an inevitable fate! The good news is that it's both preventable and treatable. We'll equip you with strategies to create a culture of self-care, including:

- **Scheduling Breaks and Disconnecting:** Regularly stepping away from work to recharge your mental and physical batteries.

- **Powering Down Before Bed:** Establishing a relaxing bedtime routine to ensure quality sleep.

- **Saying Yes to Activities You Enjoy:** Making time for hobbies and interests that bring you joy and help you de-stress.

- **Listening to Your Body:** Paying attention to warning signs like fatigue, irritability, and feeling overwhelmed.

By incorporating these practices, you'll be building a sustainable work style that fosters both productivity and well-being. Remember, a healthy and energized you is a much more successful you!

In the following sections, we'll explore the power of delegation and setting boundaries to prevent overload, and delve into creating a self-care plan that addresses different aspects of your well-being. We'll also explore real-life examples to illustrate these concepts and provide actionable tips for implementation.

Section 1

Recognizing the Signs of Burnout: Are You Running on Fumes?

Ever feel like you're constantly in overdrive? You drag yourself out of bed in the morning already exhausted, the never-ending to-do list hangs over your head like a dark cloud, and even small tasks feel like a monumental effort. Sound familiar? If so, you might be experiencing burnout.

Burnout isn't just about feeling tired. It's a state of emotional, physical, and mental exhaustion caused by prolonged or excessive stress. Think of it like your body and mind hitting the brakes because they've simply had enough. Here are some common signs of burnout to watch out for:

- **Constant Exhaustion:** You feel drained all the time, even after a good night's sleep. Simple tasks leave you feeling wiped out, and the idea of facing another workday fill you with dread.

- **Cynicism and Detachment:** The enthusiasm you once had for your work has vanished. You might start feeling cynical about your job, colleagues, or even yourself. You distance yourself emotionally and may find it hard to care about anything work-related.

- **Reduced Productivity:** Burnout often leads to a noticeable decline in your performance. You might struggle to meet deadlines, make careless mistakes, or lose focus easily. The motivation and drive you once had have simply disappeared.

These are just some of the warning signs of burnout. If you're experiencing several of these symptoms, it's crucial to take action before burnout takes a toll on your health and well-being.

The good news? Burnout is preventable and treatable. In the next section, we'll explore strategies for creating a culture of self-care to combat stress and prevent burnout. Remember, you can't pour from an empty cup! By prioritizing your well-being, you'll be better equipped to conquer your digital chaos and achieve peak performance.

Section 2

Creating a Culture of Self-Care: Recharge Your Batteries and Refuel Your Passion

Feeling like a hamster on a wheel? Running from meeting to meeting, checking emails non-stop, and sacrificing your lunch break to squeeze in one more task? This constant hustle might seem productive in the short term, but it's a recipe for burnout.

Just like your phone needs regular charging to function properly, you do too! Creating a culture of self-care is about prioritizing rest and relaxation to prevent burnout and maintain your motivation and energy levels. Think of it as an investment in your most valuable asset – yourself!

Here are some strategies to recharge your batteries and refuel your passion, focusing on different areas of well-being:

- **Physical Self-Care:**
  - **Get Moving:** Aim for at least 30 minutes of moderate-intensity exercise most days of the week. This could be anything from a brisk walk or bike ride to a yoga class or dance session. Find activities you enjoy and that fit into your schedule.

  - **Nourish Your Body:** Eat a balanced diet rich in fruits, vegetables, whole grains, and lean protein. Avoid processed foods and sugary drinks that can leave you feeling sluggish. Stay

hydrated by drinking plenty of water throughout the day.

- **Get Enough Sleep:** Most adults need around 7-8 hours of sleep per night. Establish a regular sleep schedule and create a relaxing bedtime routine to ensure quality sleep.

- **Mental Self-Care:**
  - **Practice Mindfulness:** Take some time each day to focus on the present moment. Mindfulness meditation can help reduce stress, improve focus, and boost overall well-being. There are many free meditation apps available to help you get started.

  - **Challenge Your Brain:** Learning new things keeps your mind sharp and engaged. Take an online course, read a book on a new topic, or try a brain-training app.

  - **Spend Time in Nature:** Immerse yourself in the beauty of nature. Go for a walk in the park, hike in the woods, or simply sit outside and enjoy the fresh air. Spending time in nature has been shown to reduce stress levels and improve mood.

- **Emotional Self-Care:**
  - **Connect with Loved Ones:** Make time for the people who matter most to you. Social connection is essential for emotional well-being. Schedule regular calls or video chats with friends and family, or plan outings for quality time together.

- **Express Yourself Creatively:** Engage in activities that allow you to express yourself creatively. This could be anything from painting or drawing to writing, playing music, or dancing.

- **Do Something You Enjoy:** Schedule time for activities that bring you joy and relaxation. This could be anything from reading a book to listening to music, taking a warm bath, or spending time on a favourite hobby.

By incorporating these strategies into your daily routine, you'll be creating a sustainable work style that allows you to be productive without sacrificing your well-being. Remember, a well-rested and recharged you is a much more productive and successful you! In the next section, we'll explore the power of delegation and setting boundaries to prevent overload and burnout.

Self-Care Checklist

Track your progress by checking off each box as you complete the activity!

Area	Activity	Weekly Target
Recharge Your Body	Move your body for 30 minutes	☐ 3 times a week
Recharge Your Body	Eat a healthy breakfast	☐ Every day
Recharge Your Body	Pack a healthy lunch	☐ Most weekdays

Area	Activity	Weekly Target
Recharge Your Body	Drink plenty of water throughout the day	☐ Aim for 8 glasses
Recharge Your Body	Go to bed at a consistent time and aim for 7-8 hours of sleep	☐ Every night
Sharpen Your Mind	Dedicate 10 minutes each day to mindfulness meditation	☐ Every day
Sharpen Your Mind	Read a book on a topic that interests you for 30 minutes	☐ 3 times a week
Sharpen Your Mind	Learn a new skill by taking an online course or watching educational videos	☐ Once a week
Sharpen Your Mind	Spend time in nature	☐ At least once a week
Nurture Your Spirit	Connect with loved ones	☐ Once a week
Nurture Your Spirit	Pursue a creative hobby	☐ A few times a week
Nurture Your Spirit	Do something you enjoy every day	☐ Every day

By incorporating these strategies into your daily routine, you'll be creating a sustainable work style that allows you to be productive without sacrificing your well-being. Remember, a well-rested and recharged you is a much more productive and successful you!

Section 3

The Power of Delegation and Saying No: Stop Trying to Do It All

We've all been there. The never-ending to-do list keeps growing, your inbox explodes with new requests, and you feel like you're drowning in a sea of tasks. The pressure to do it all can be overwhelming, but here's the secret: you don't have to be a one-person show!

Delegation and saying no are powerful tools that can help you avoid overload and prevent burnout.

Delegation: Sharing the Workload
Delegation isn't about dumping tasks on someone else; it's about empowering your team and maximizing everyone's strengths. Here's why delegation is your friend:

- **Frees Up Your Time:** By delegating tasks that can be handled by others, you free up your time to focus on higher-level priorities that require your specific expertise.

- **Boosts Team Morale:** When you trust colleagues with tasks, it shows you value their skills and contributions. This can lead to increased motivation and a more engaged team.

- **Develops Talent:** Delegation provides opportunities for team members to learn and grow by taking on new challenges.

Saying No: Setting Boundaries

Saying no isn't about being negative or unhelpful. It's about setting healthy boundaries and protecting your time and energy. Here's how to say no gracefully:

- **Be Clear and Concise:** Explain politely that you have too much on your plate at the moment. Offer to help in another way or suggest someone else who might be able to assist.

- **Focus on Solutions:** If possible, suggest an alternative solution or offer to take on the task at a later date.

- **Don't Feel Guilty:** It's okay to prioritize your workload and well-being. By saying no, you're ensuring you can deliver high-quality work on the commitments you already have.

Taking Control of Your Workload:

In addition to delegation and saying no, here are some strategies to take control of your workload and prevent burnout:

- **Regularly Assess Your Stress Levels:** Don't wait until you're on the verge of collapse to recognize stress. Pay attention to your body's warning signs, such as headaches, fatigue, or irritability. There are many stress-management apps available to help you track your stress levels and identify healthy coping mechanisms.

- **Schedule Breaks:** Our brains aren't designed for constant focus. Schedule short breaks throughout the day to get up and move around, clear your head, and recharge your batteries. Even a few minutes can make a big difference in your energy levels and productivity.

- **Schedule Time for Activities You Enjoy:** Make time for activities that bring you joy and help you de-stress. This could be anything from spending time with loved ones to pursuing a hobby, taking a relaxing bath, or simply enjoying some time in nature. Scheduling these activities into your calendar ensures you prioritize your well-being.

Real-Life Example:
Anjali, a marketing manager, was constantly overwhelmed with a never-ending list of tasks. She felt pressured to do everything herself and was on the verge of burnout. She learned the power of delegation and started assigning tasks to her team members based on their skills. Anjali also started politely declining requests that fell outside her core responsibilities. By delegating and setting boundaries, Anjali was able to regain control of her workload, reduce her stress levels, and improve her overall well-being.

Remember: You are not a superhero! Delegation and saying no are essential tools for maintaining a healthy work-life balance and preventing burnout. In the next section, we'll provide actionable tips on how to delegate effectively and politely decline requests.

The Case of Clara: From Burnout to Balance

Clara, a passionate and dedicated marketing manager, thrived on the fast-paced environment of her company. However, her dedication turned into a double-edged sword. She constantly felt the pressure to perform, taking on more and more tasks without ever saying no. Working long hours and neglecting breaks became the norm. While she initially felt productive, this unsustainable approach slowly chipped away at her well-being.

The warning signs started subtly. Clara found herself constantly tired, easily irritated, and struggling to focus. Work that used to be stimulating felt overwhelming. The joy she once had for her job began to fade. One day, overwhelmed by a looming deadline and facing a mountain of unfinished tasks, Clara broke down in tears. It was a wake-up call.

Clara realized she was on the path to burnout. She sought guidance from a therapist who emphasized the importance of self-care and a healthy work-life balance. Clara started implementing changes, one step at a time. She began scheduling regular breaks throughout the day, even if it was just for a quick walk or some deep breathing exercises. She also embraced the power of delegation, identifying tasks that could be effectively handled by her team members. At first, it felt counterintuitive to "give up" control, but Clara quickly realized that a well-delegated task freed up her time to focus on higher-level priorities.

Saying no became another important tool. Clara politely declined requests that fell outside her core responsibilities or would overload her schedule. She learned to prioritize her well-being, carving out time for activities she enjoyed, like yoga and spending time with friends. These changes weren't easy, but the results were undeniable.

Gradually, Clara felt a shift. Her energy levels increased, her focus sharpened, and her creativity blossomed. She felt more engaged at work and her relationships with colleagues improved. Most importantly, Clara rediscovered the passion and joy she once had for her job.

Clara's story is a powerful reminder that neglecting self-care can lead to burnout. By prioritizing your well-being, delegating tasks effectively, and setting healthy boundaries, you can achieve a sustainable work-life balance and maintain your motivation for the long haul.

Chapter 10

Crafting Your Action Plan: A Roadmap to Conquer Your Chaos

Congratulations! You've reached a pivotal point in your journey to digital detox. We've explored the root causes of digital chaos, unpacked powerful strategies for managing distractions, and emphasized the importance of prioritizing well-being. Now it's time to translate this knowledge into action.

This chapter is all about crafting your personalized **action plan**, your very own roadmap to finally conquer digital chaos and achieve the peace of mind and productivity you deserve. Think of it as a battle plan, tailored to your unique needs and challenges.

Here's a sneak peek of what awaits you:

- **Reviewing Key Concepts:** We'll take a quick moment to refresh your memory on the arsenal of powerful tools you've accumulated throughout this book.

- **Developing Your Personalized Plan:** We'll guide you through a step-by-step process of building your action plan, including setting SMART goals, choosing the most effective strategies, and creating a system for tracking progress.

- **Creating a Support System:** Let's face it, conquering digital chaos is a marathon, not a sprint. We'll discuss the importance of building a support system to keep you motivated and accountable.

- **Conquer Your Chaos: Action Plan Template:** We've included a downloadable template to help you translate theory into action. This comprehensive guide will walk you through defining your challenges, setting SMART goals, outlining action steps, and establishing a tracking system for sustainable success.

- **From Chaos to Calm: Sarah's Story:** Meet Sarah, a real-life example of someone who successfully conquered digital chaos using the strategies outlined in this book. We'll explore the specific techniques she implemented and the positive impact they had on her productivity, stress levels, and overall well-being.

Remember, this is *your* action plan. Don't be afraid to customize it, experiment, and find what works best for you. With dedication and the right tools in your arsenal, you can finally silence the digital noise and achieve a calmer, more productive you!

Are you ready to take control? Let's dive in!

Section 1

Reviewing Key Concepts: Your Digital Detox Toolkit

Phew, we've covered a lot of ground on our journey to conquering digital chaos! Just to refresh your memory, here's a quick recap of the powerful tools you've collected in your digital detox toolkit:

- **Taming the Inbox:** We learned strategies to manage email overload, including techniques for prioritizing messages, utilizing filters, and scheduling dedicated times to check your inbox.

- **Outsmarting Distractions:** You discovered ways to identify and minimize digital distractions, such as implementing timeboxing for focused work sessions, utilizing website blockers, and silencing notifications.

- **The Power of Prioritization:** We explored effective methods for prioritizing tasks, like creating to-do lists using the Eisenhower Matrix, setting realistic deadlines, and saying "no" to requests that overload your schedule.

- **Embracing Self-Care:** You learned the importance of prioritizing your well-being to combat stress and burnout. This included techniques for getting enough sleep, taking regular breaks, and incorporating physical activity and mindfulness practices into your daily routine.

- **Technology for Good:** We discussed how to leverage technology to your advantage, exploring productivity apps for time management, project organization, and communication.

Remember, this is just a quick refresher! These are all valuable tools you can use to customize your own action plan and finally conquer the digital chaos that's been holding you back.

Section 2

Developing Your Personalized Plan: Your Roadmap to Freedom

Now that you've got a toolbox full of powerful strategies, it's time to build your personalized action plan! Think of it as your roadmap to finally conquer digital chaos and achieve the peace of mind and productivity you deserve.

Here's how to get started:

Step 1: Reflect and Prioritize:

- **Grab a pen and paper (or your favourite note-taking app) and brainstorm!** Jot down the areas in your digital life that cause you the most stress and overwhelm. Is it a constantly overflowing inbox? Social media rabbit holes? The never-ending stream of notifications?

- **Be honest with yourself:** Identify your biggest digital distractions and the areas where you feel you lose the most time.

- **Prioritize your battles:** Once you have your list, pick the 2-3 areas that are causing you the most pain. Trying to tackle everything at once can be overwhelming. Focus on making significant progress in a few key areas first.

Step 2: Set SMART Goals:

SMART goals are like lighthouses guiding you towards success. They're:

- **Specific:** What exactly do you want to achieve? Instead of "check email less," aim for "check email only twice a day during designated times."

- **Measurable:** How will you track your progress? This could be the number of times you check your phone per day, the amount of time you spend focused work sessions, or the number of completed tasks on your to-do list.

- **Achievable:** Be realistic about what you can accomplish. Aim for goals that are challenging but achievable within a specific timeframe.

- **Relevant:** Do your goals align with your overall desire to conquer digital chaos? Make sure they're relevant to the areas you identified as priorities.

- **Time-bound:** Set a specific timeframe for achieving your goals. This will help you stay on track and motivated.

Step 3: Choose Your Weapons:
Remember the awesome strategies you learned throughout this book? Now's the time to pick the ones that will be most effective for you!

- **Taming the Inbox:** Will you use filters and labels or schedule dedicated "email time" slots?

- **Outsmarting Distractions:** Will you try timeboxing for focused work sessions, utilize website blockers, or silence notifications?

- **The Power of Prioritization:** Will you create to-do lists using the Eisenhower Matrix, set realistic deadlines, or learn to say "no" more effectively?

- **Embracing Self-Care:** How will you prioritize your well-being? Will you schedule regular breaks for walks or meditation, or aim for a consistent sleep schedule?

Bonus Tip: Don't be afraid to experiment! Find the strategies and tools that work best for your unique work style and preferences.

Ready to get started?
"Action Plan Template" (provided end of this chapter). It will guide you through the process of crafting your personalized plan to finally conquer digital chaos and achieve lasting peace of mind.

Section 3

Creating a Support System: Your Cheer Squad for Success

Let's face it, changing habits and conquering digital chaos can be tough. We all have those days where willpower crumbles, and we fall back into old patterns. That's why having a strong support system is crucial for lasting change. Think of it as your personal cheer squad, there to keep you motivated, accountable, and celebrating your victories along the way.

Here's why a support system rocks:
- **Accountability is a Game Changer:** Knowing someone is checking in on your progress can be a powerful motivator. It helps you stay committed to your goals and prevents those sneaky moments of "I'll just do it tomorrow."

- **Sharing is Caring:** Talking about your struggles and triumphs with others who understand can be incredibly helpful. They can offer encouragement, share their own experiences, and help you brainstorm solutions to challenges.

- **Celebrating Milestones:** Conquering digital chaos is a journey filled with wins, big and small. Having a support system allows you to celebrate these victories, no matter how seemingly insignificant. This keeps you motivated and reminds you how far you've come.

Ready to build your squad? Here are some ideas:
- **Find an Accountability Partner:** This could be a colleague, friend, or family member who's also looking to improve their digital habits. Schedule regular check-ins to discuss your goals, challenges, and progress.

- **Join a Productivity Group:** There are online and in-person communities dedicated to productivity and reducing digital overwhelm. These groups offer a wealth of support, resources, and shared experiences.

- **Consider a Productivity Coach or Therapist:** A professional can provide personalized guidance, help you identify underlying issues, and develop strategies for long-term success.

Remember, your support system doesn't have to be complicated. The most important thing is to find people who believe in you and your ability to conquer digital chaos!

Conduct a Self-Assessment:
In addition to brainstorming your pain points, include prompts like:
- When do I feel most overwhelmed by digital distractions? (During work? Scrolling social media at night?)

- How much time do I realistically spend on activities that don't contribute to my goals? (Track phone usage for a day or estimate time spent on social media/games)

- What aspects of my digital life leave me feeling drained or stressed? (Constant notifications? Information overload?)

Conquer Your Chaos: Action Plan Template

Name: _____
Date: _____

My Biggest Digital Challenges:
- Briefly list 2-3 areas in your digital life that cause you the most stress and overwhelm.
- Be specific! (e.g., constantly overflowing inbox, social media distractions, notification overload)

SMART Goals:
- Fill out the chart below for each of your challenges, setting specific, measurable, achievable, relevant, and time-bound goals for improvement.

Challenge	Specific Goal	Measurable	Achievable	Relevant	Time-Bound
Challenge 1	(e.g., Reduce email checking to 2 times per day)	(e.g., Track the number of times I check email daily)	(Yes/No)	(Yes/No)	(e.g., By next week)
Challenge 2					
Challenge 3					

Action Steps:
- For each challenge, list the specific strategies you will use to achieve your goals.
- Refer back to the strategies covered in the book (e.g., timeboxing for focused work, utilizing website blockers, creating to-do lists using the Eisenhower Matrix).

Challenge	Action Steps
Challenge 1	(e.g., Schedule dedicated "email time" slots, utilize email filters)
Challenge 2	
Challenge 3	

Support System:
- List the names and contact information of your accountability partners, support groups (e.g., weekly or bi-weekly calls, virtual co-working sessions), or therapist (if applicable).

Tracking Progress: Choose a method (or a combination of methods) to track your progress and celebrate milestones.

Here are some ideas:
- **"Habit Tracker Apps:** Utilize apps designed to track habits like focused work sessions, time spent on specific apps, or completing daily tasks.

- **Daily/Weekly Journal Entries:** Dedicate time each day or week to reflect on your digital habits and progress towards your goals. Note challenges and areas for improvement.

- **Progress Chart:** Create a visual chart to track your progress over time. This could involve logging the number of times you achieve your goals (e.g., checking email only twice a day) or the amount of time you spend on focused work sessions.

- **celebrate milestones**: Briefly mention other tracking methods like using a productivity spreadsheet or a dedicated "wins" list to celebrate milestones (both big and small).

Remember:
- Review your action plan regularly and adjust as needed.
- Celebrate your victories, big and small!
- Don't be discouraged by setbacks – just pick yourself up and keep moving forward.

Bonus Tip:
- Schedule regular check-ins with your accountability partner or support group to discuss your progress and stay motivated.

This template is just a starting point! Feel free to customize it to fit your specific needs and preferences.

From Chaos to Calm: Julie's Story
Julie, a marketing manager at a bustling tech startup, knew something had to change. Her workday was a constant battle against email notifications, social media feeds, and colleagues' pings. Tasks piled up, deadlines loomed, and a nagging feeling of overwhelm followed her everywhere.

Determined to reclaim control, Julie stumbled upon this book. The concept of "digital detox" resonated deeply. She realized her constant connectivity was hindering her productivity and well-being. Armed with the strategies she learned; Julie embarked on her journey to conquer digital chaos.

Taking Back Control:
- **Timeboxing:** Julie started by implementing timeboxing. She blocked out specific time slots for focused work sessions, free from distractions. This allowed her to tackle tasks efficiently and avoid feeling overwhelmed by her to-do list.

- **Focus Apps:** To minimize distractions during these focused work sessions, Julie downloaded a focus app. This app blocked distracting websites and social media, allowing her to stay present and truly get things done.

- **Mindfulness for Managing Stress:** Recognizing the impact of digital overload on her stress levels, Julie adopted a short daily mindfulness practice. Taking just 10 minutes each morning to focus on her breath and clear her mind helped her approach her day with a calmer, more centred perspective.

The Road to Success:
The changes weren't easy at first. There were moments of temptation to slip back into old habits. But, Julie persevered, and the results were undeniable.

- **Increased Productivity:** With focused work sessions and fewer distractions, Julie found she could accomplish more in less time. Her to-do list started shrinking, and a sense of accomplishment replaced the constant feeling of being behind.

- **Reduced Stress:** The mindfulness practice equipped Julie with tools to manage stress throughout the workday. She felt calmer and more in control, even during hectic periods.

- **Improved Work-Life Balance:** Setting boundaries with technology allowed Julie to truly disconnect after work. She could be present with family and friends without the constant urge to check her phone.

Julie's story is a testament to the power of the strategies outlined in this book. By taking control of her digital habits, Sarah transformed her work life and overall well-being. You too can conquer digital chaos and achieve a calmer, more productive you!

Conclusion

Reclaim Your Time, Reimagine Your Potential

Congratulations! You've reached the end of your journey to conquer digital chaos. Throughout this book, we've explored the challenges of our hyper-connected world and unpacked powerful strategies for taking back control.

Key Takeaways:
- **Digital overwhelm is real, but it's not inevitable.** You have the power to transform your relationship with technology and create a digital landscape that empowers you, not hinders you.

- **A focus on well-being is crucial for long-term success.** Prioritizing self-care and mindfulness equips you with the resilience to navigate the demands of the digital age.

- **There's no one-size-fits-all solution.** Experiment with the strategies covered in this book and discover what works best for your unique needs and preferences.

- **Building a support system is essential for lasting change.** Surround yourself with accountability partners and communities that understand your goals and celebrate your victories.

Your Digital Transformation Awaits
Don't let this be the end of your journey. Now is the time to take action! Use the tools and strategies you've learned to craft your personalized plan and begin conquering your

digital chaos. Remember, change takes time and commitment. There will be setbacks, but with perseverance and a supportive community, you can achieve lasting success.

Feeling swamped by the digital world? Don't go it alone! Our supportive community awaits at unleash369@proton.me . We offer a collection of resources and templates to tame the digital chaos, along with ongoing tips and challenges to keep you sharp. Find inspiration from real stories of others conquering the digital beast, and connect with a network of like-minded individuals for encouragement and accountability. Take charge of your digital life – join us today!

Remember, you are not alone in this digital age. We are here to support you on your journey to a calmer, more productive, and fulfilling life! Embrace the power of taking control of your digital habits and watch your productivity soar.

www.ingramcontent.com/pod-product-compliance
Lightning Source LLC
Chambersburg PA
CBHW050107230526
45470CB00004B/1720